State Science and Technology Policy Advice

ISSUES, OPPORTUNITIES, AND CHALLENGES

Summary of a National Convocation

Steve Olson, *Rapporteur*
Jay B. Labov, *Editor*

NATIONAL ACADEMY OF SCIENCES,
NATIONAL ACADEMY OF ENGINEERING, AND
INSTITUTE OF MEDICINE
OF THE NATIONAL ACADEMIES

D1364051

THE NATIONAL ACADEMIES PRESS
Washington, D.C.
www.nap.edu

THE NATIONAL ACADEMIES PRESS   500 Fifth Street, N.W.   Washington, DC 20001

This study was supported by the Arnold and Mabel Beckman Fund of the National Academy of Sciences and the National Academy of Engineering. Any opinions, findings, and conclusions or recommendations expressed in this publication are those of the persons identified in the report and do not necessarily reflect the views of the National Academies.

International Standard Book Number-13:   978-0-309-11711-1
International Standard Book Number-10:   0-309-11711-9

Additional copies of this report are available from the National Academies Press, 500 Fifth Street, N.W., Lockbox 285, Washington, DC 20055; (800) 624-6242 or (202)334-3313 (in the Washington metropolitan area); Internet, http://www.nap.edu.

Suggested citation: National Academy of Sciences, National Academy of Engineering, and Institute of Medicine. (2008). *State Science and Technology Policy Advice: Issues, Opportunities, and Challenges: Summary of a National Convocation.* Steve Olson, Rapporteur. Jay B. Labov, Editor. Washington, DC: The National Academies Press.

THE NATIONAL ACADEMIES
Advisers to the Nation on Science, Engineering, and Medicine

The **National Academy of Sciences** is a private, nonprofit, self-perpetuating society of distinguished scholars engaged in scientific and engineering research, dedicated to the furtherance of science and technology and to their use for the general welfare. Upon the authority of the charter granted to it by the Congress in 1863, the Academy has a mandate that requires it to advise the federal government on scientific and technical matters. Dr. Ralph J. Cicerone is president of the National Academy of Sciences.

The **National Academy of Engineering** was established in 1964, under the charter of the National Academy of Sciences, as a parallel organization of outstanding engineers. It is autonomous in its administration and in the selection of its members, sharing with the National Academy of Sciences the responsibility for advising the federal government. The National Academy of Engineering also sponsors engineering programs aimed at meeting national needs, encourages education and research, and recognizes the superior achievements of engineers. Dr. Charles M. Vest is president of the National Academy of Engineering.

The **Institute of Medicine** was established in 1970 by the National Academy of Sciences to secure the services of eminent members of appropriate professions in the examination of policy matters pertaining to the health of the public. The Institute acts under the responsibility given to the National Academy of Sciences by its congressional charter to be an adviser to the federal government and, upon its own initiative, to identify issues of medical care, research, and education. Dr. Harvey V. Fineberg is president of the Institute of Medicine.

The **National Research Council** was organized by the National Academy of Sciences in 1916 to associate the broad community of science and technology with the Academy's purposes of furthering knowledge and advising the federal government. Functioning in accordance with general policies determined by the Academy, the Council has become the principal operating agency of both the National Academy of Sciences and the National Academy of Engineering in providing services to the government, the public, and the scientific and engineering communities. The Council is administered jointly by both Academies and the Institute of Medicine. Dr. Ralph J. Cicerone and Dr. Charles M. Vest are chair and vice chair, respectively, of the National Research Council.

www.national-academies.org

CONVOCATION ORGANIZERS

Deborah Johnson Benoit, Executive Assistant, National Academy of Sciences

Jay Cole, Education Policy Advisor to the Governor of West Virginia and Christine Mirzayan Policy Fellow, National Academies

Lynn E. Elfner, Chief Executive Director, The Ohio Academy of Science

Nancy F. Huddleston, Senior Communications Officer, Division of Earth and Life Studies, National Research Council

Jay B. Labov (*Convocation Director*), Senior Advisor for Education and Communication, National Academy of Sciences

Karl S. Pister,* Chancellor Emeritus, University of California, Santa Cruz

Donna Gerardi Riordan, Director of Programs, California Council on Science and Technology

---

*Member, National Academy of Engineering.

Contents

Preface

"*The United States is entering a new era of scientific and technological development, one where the states assume a much greater role than has been the case in the past. We are fairly early in the history of the state science and technology policy movement, and recognizing this also allows us in a sense to recognize that we're making this history. We're in uncharted territory, and we need to learn from everything we're doing so that we continue to make progress in the future.*"
—Jay Cole, West Virginia education advisor, in the closing session of the convocation

Since the 1945 publication of Vannevar Bush's *Science—The Endless Frontier*, the federal government has played the predominant role in supporting research and development (R&D) and in establishing public policies that affect science and technology (S&T) in the United States. That role remains vitally important today. Almost every major policy issue is influenced by scientific and technological information and expertise. There remains a clear and ongoing mandate for a cohesive set of federal policy and programs that both sustain R&D and promote the application of new knowledge.

But the federal government is no longer the sole focus of R&D funding and S&T policy making. As the influence of scientific and engineering research on daily life has steadily increased, the states have assumed an increasing responsibility for developing, formalizing, and institutionalizing policies and programs that support R&D and enable S&T evidence and expertise to be incorporated into policy making. And as the federal government faces continuing budget shortfalls and a (one hopes, temporary) reluctance to enact policies based on scientific evidence, the roles of the states are likely to expand.

Today there are a great range and diversity of approaches for incorporating scientific and technological advice and evidence into policy and decision making at the state level. Many states fund research directly, much of it tied to driving economic opportunity within the state. Some governors have science advisors, and others do not. Many states rely on consultation with experts from academia, government, and industry. Some have formal arrangements with their universities to conduct research for parts of the state government, such as the regulatory agencies that work to protect public health and safety or to manage the state's infrastructure and natural resources.

At the national level, the federal government can rely on various organizations, such as the national laboratories and the nonpartisan, private, and nonprofit National Academies, for advice. However, as states make an increasing number of S&T-based policy decisions, much more needs to be done to develop rational, collaborative strategies for using S&T information and expertise at the state level. A key emphasis would be to develop stronger, ongoing relationships among governmental officials, individual scientists and engineers, and state and federal scientific organizations (such as state academies of science).

It is clear that high-quality scientific information and evidence can improve policy decisions on everything from environmental protection to education to energy to health care. However, in the current policy-making environment, science and technology compete with the panoply of other ideas and voices surrounding a given policy development. Oftentimes, a lack of scientific information is not the problem—rather the problem is where to turn for trusted information. State officials must be able to trust the advice and information they receive and must be able to distinguish among and reconcile competing claims.

Even if information exists, it may not be useful or meaningful to recipients of that information. In general, scientists and engineers have done a poor job of communicating scientific information clearly and effectively to policy makers and the public. Scientific information is useful for policy making only if it is presented in a timely fashion and in the context of the many political and economic factors that policy makers must also consider. Clear science communication is especially important given that only a small fraction of the citizen law-makers who are elected to state legislatures and the people who advise governors or regulatory agencies have a background in science or technology.

There is a growing need for state officials and the scientific and engineering communities to find ways to communicate with each other, to share ideas and effective practices, and to work together both within their states and across regions to realize the benefits and efficiencies of collaboration. Cooperation and joint decision making across state lines has proven even more difficult than working within individual states. The current ad hoc system of state-level S&T policy advice cannot meet the needs that exist.

ADDRESSING THE CHALLENGES: A NEW APPROACH

These issues were explored during a first-of-its-kind National Convocation on the Roles of Science and Technology in State-Level Policy Making that was held October 15-16, 2007, at the Arnold and Mabel Beckman Center in Irvine, California. The convocation was organized by the National Academy of Sciences, the National Academy of Engineering, and the Institute of Medicine in collaboration with the National Association of Academies of Science and the California Council on Science and Technology. Additional information about all of these organizations is provided in the body of this summary.

The convocation had several major goals:

1. To discuss with state policy makers the benefits that can result from policies that are informed by science and technology.
2. To better understand the needs, opportunities, and constraints of decision makers in the legislative and executive branches of state governments for integrating advice from the science and technology community.
3. To examine current models for involving science and technical expertise in state policy making.
4. To explore ways that the National Academies might
   a. expand its relationships with states in providing advice directly to them and
   b. learn from state officials and organizations about issues and concerns that would enable the National Research Council to undertake studies that are more directly applicable to the needs of states.
5. To begin development of a network of state and national policy makers interested in science and technology issues, plan an agenda for future meetings and related activities, establish a plan for communication with others who should be involved with these efforts, and explore sources of funding to sustain such a network.

Scientists, engineers, state policy makers, experts from state regulatory agencies, representatives from foundations, and experts in scientific communication from twenty states and the District of Columbia participated in this event (see Figure P-1).

The convocation enabled participants to explore the contributions and relationships of science and technology to state policy making from a variety of perspectives. On the morning of the first day, the keynote address offered a historical perspective of federal R&D policy and spending and its possible effects on policy making at the state level. Using a report from the Pew Center on the States as a point of departure, convocation participants next explored the variable landscape of state S&T policy-making practices that are in place today. This presentation was followed by a case study of state and regional policy making involving the watershed of the Columbia River Basin and how authoritative scientific advice (in this case from the National Research Council) helped to overcome policy making gridlock in Washington State. Representatives from several state and national organizations, including the Ohio Academy of Science, the California Council on Science and Technology, the National Research Council, and the federal laboratories, described the kinds of policy-related information and advice they can provide state officials and offered examples of successful interactions.

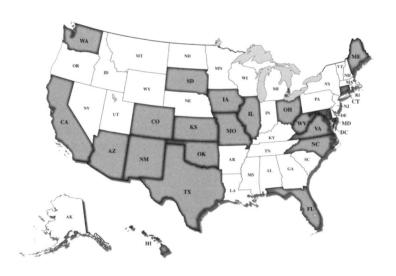

FIGURE P-1 States (shaded) represented at the national convocation.

The afternoon sessions on the first day began with talks by representatives from the executive and legislative branches of New Mexico and West Virginia, respectively, the National Conference of State Legislatures, and an environmental regulatory agency in Texas, all of whom described the challenges they face when trying to gather and then incorporate scientific information and advice into their work. During much of the remainder of the afternoon, convocation participants from multiple sectors and regions of the country convened in breakout sessions to discuss what they had heard and how that information might be applied to addressing problems related specifically to energy and the environment.

The second day focused on ways to improve communication between policy makers and scientists, engineers, and other individuals with technical training. A panel consisting of a social science researcher who has focused on communicating science, a science reporter from the *Los Angeles Times*, an engineering professor who also produces and delivers a weekly broadcast about engineering on public radio, and an expert in transmitting scientific information to policy makers and the public engaged the other participants in a spirited discussion about how to most effectively communicate S&T information and evidence to state policy makers. Participants then assembled into small working groups based on their geographic location to plan for future regional events and to offer advice to the organizers of the convocation about possible topics for future convocations.

STRUCTURE OF THE SUMMARY

This summary is written as a narrative rather than as a chronological account of the convocation. It highlights the major themes that emerged from the presentations and from the rich discussions that occurred in both plenary and breakout sessions. Quotations come from a transcript of the speakers' comments that were recorded during the plenary sessions, and the summary draws on PowerPoint presentations and other materials distributed prior to and during the event.

The agenda, which lists the plenary and breakout sessions in the order in which they occurred, appears in Appendix A. The diversity of interests and expertise of convocation presenters and participants is evident from the list of participants and their institutional affiliations, which appears in Appendix B. Biographical sketches of the planning committee members and the convocation presenters appear in Appendix C. Readers are encouraged to contact individual speakers if they wish to obtain additional information about any of the points in this summary. Access to all PowerPoint presentations is available through links on the National Convocation website at: <http://nasonline.org/convocation>.

On issues ranging from energy to air quality to natural resources to education, state and local policy makers are unquestionably making more and more decisions that affect all of us on a daily basis. This convocation was an important step toward both recognizing S&T information as an important element of policy making and establishing the networks that will be necessary to bring S&T experts and state policy makers together in more meaningful ways.

Karl S. Pister
Chair, Board of Directors,
California Council on Science and Technology
Dean and Roy W. Carlson Professor of Engineering Emeritus,
University of California, Berkeley

Acknowledgments

This convocation summary has been reviewed in draft form by individuals chosen for their diverse perspectives and technical expertise. The purpose of this independent review is to provide candid and critical comments that will assist the institution in making its published report as sound as possible and to ensure that the summary meets institutional standards for objectivity, evidence, and responsiveness to the charge. The review comments and draft manuscript remain confidential to protect the integrity of the process. We thank the following individuals for their review of this report: Jennifer Mendez, Governmental Issues, Carpet and Rug Institute, Arlington, VA; Douglas M. Smith, State Senator, District 27, Dover-Foxcroft, ME; and Mary Jo Waits, Pew Center on the States, The Pew Charitable Trusts, Washington, DC.

Although the reviewers listed above provided many constructive comments and suggestions, they were not asked to endorse the content of the report nor did they see the final draft of the report before its release. The review of this report was overseen by Dr. Peter Bruns, Howard Hughes Medical Institute, Chevy Chase, MD. He was responsible for making certain that an independent examination of this summary was carried out in accordance with institutional procedures and that all review comments were carefully considered. Responsibility for the final content of this summary rests entirely with the author(s) and the institution.

1

The Need for Science and Technology Policy Advice at the State Level

In the past, cities and states became powerful in large part because of their locations, their access to natural resources, and the skills of their workforces. If a city was located next to a navigable river, it could build on its strengths as a transportation hub. If an area had plentiful coal or oil resources, it could become a center of energy production.

In the United States today, the importance of location and natural resources has diminished. The vital factors that now generate comparative advantage are "created, not inherited," said Doug Henton, the president of Comparative Economics and an expert on economic development at the national, regional, state, and local levels. For example, Silicon Valley was essentially a fruit-growing region, Henton pointed out, until a handful of companies initiated the microelectronics revolution there. Starbucks became successful when it developed a way of giving its customers an experience that would justify paying much more for coffee than if they made the coffee themselves. "It's not just about technology," said Henton.

Today, value is created through talented people, an entrepreneurial culture, networks, world-class universities, and other institutional, cultural, and technological attributes. "It's about the venture capitalists, it's about the networks, it's about the underlying support system—the lawyers, the accountants—all those people working together to create companies and take ideas to market," Henton said.

Talented people and a skilled workforce are the products of education, which is why good schools, colleges, and universities are so important to the economic and social prospects of cities, states, and nations. Financial capital flows to wherever good ideas are located, and information is largely free and globally distributed in the age of Google. But "you have to have people who know how to use [information]," Henton said. "That's the know-how—people who know how to put things together."

These trends will intensify in the 21st century. If the United States is to compete with other countries, it must do so on the basis of high-value products and services, "and that's going to require innovation," according to Henton. Routine work will be done by machines or by low-paid workers. For the United States to remain a high-wage country, it must be a center of innovation, in part through the education, training, and preparation of its workforce.

The United States has had the strongest system of higher education in the world for more than half a century, said Karl Pister, a member of the National Academy of Engineering, chair of the Board of Directors for the California Council on Science and Technology, and Dean and Roy W. Carlson professor of engineering emeritus at the University of California, Berkeley. The nation also has a very strong system of laboratories supported by the federal government. Universities and federal laboratories both have had great success transferring ideas and technologies to the private sector.

But colleges, universities, and federal laboratories have had much less success providing scientific and technical advice to policy makers. "Providing sound science and technology policy advice in a form that is understandable and actionable by elected officials remains a challenge," Pister said.

This weakness is particularly evident at the state level. According to Richard Atkinson, president emeritus of the University of California system, a "glaring failure" of the U.S. science and technology system has been "the absence of science and technology input at the state and regional level. . . . There is no end of examples of policies that have been established at the state level that have failed dramatically because they have not taken into account science and technology issues."[1]

Yet science and technology are having an ever-greater influence on state policies. As Matt Sundeen, program principal of the National Conference of State Legislators said, "All the leading public policy issues have some sort of science component, whether it's energy policy, stem cell research, or education. You can make a case that almost everything

---

[1]An example of a national health policy that was compromised because science was not adequately considered is provided in this summary at the beginning of the section entitled "When Scientists Take a Stand" on page 48.

has some sort of science and technology component to it, and therefore [science and technology] should be important to state legislators."

These state policies, in turn, can have a dramatic influence on everyone's lives. As the federal government becomes increasingly constrained because of other commitments and political disputes, states and localities have unprecedented opportunities to use science and technology in productive ways. "Now that I'm working at the state level in California, I realize that the policy decisions that really impact our personal lives and our schools and our communities happen at the state level," said Donna Gerardi Riordan, director of programs of the California Council on Science and Technology, who worked at the National Research Council in Washington, DC, before moving to California. "Given that we have a rich resource of science and technology expertise in almost every community in the nation, there's an opportunity to bring that expertise to bear on the decisions that affect all of us at a very local and very personal level."

People who are interested in science and technology have tremendous potential to influence state policies, but today that potential is largely unrealized. At the same time, many of the institutional structures and personal relationships needed to inject scientific and technological considerations into state policy making already exist. Participants at the convocation focused on how to use these structures and relationships to build a strong state science and technology policy advising system that could have great benefits for all citizens.

2

The National Context for Science and Technology Policy Advice

S tate policy making takes place in a national context, and many state efforts build on federal activities or models. At the convocation, Richard Atkinson provided a historical overview of science and technology policy advice at the federal level, dividing his analysis into four periods: before the 1940s, the decade of the 1940s, the period from 1950 until 1975, and the period from 1975 until the present (summarized in Table 2-1).

HISTORICAL OVERVIEW

Before World War II, federal industrial laboratories in the United States conducted "brilliant research," Atkinson said, but most of this research was focused on commercial applications of new knowledge. Perhaps a dozen U.S. universities and a few private nonprofit institutions, such as the Carnegie Institution of Washington, could be considered world-class research institutions, but these institutions received virtually no funding from the federal government. Instead, they relied on their endowments, private fundraising, some funding from industry, and state funds. Before 1940, said Atkinson, researchers in private industry and even in universities "depended very much on the Europeans for basic research."

As it became clear that the United States would soon become embroiled in World War II, President Franklin D. Roosevelt established the National Defense Research Council (NDRC) in 1940 to organize the nation's scientific resources for wartime. The NDRC was chaired by Vannevar Bush,

TABLE 2-1 Significant Dates and Events in Federal Funding of Science and Technology

Pre-1940s	1940-1949	1950-1975	1976-Present
Research on commercial applications of knowledge by federal industrial laboratories. Funding from endowments, private fundraising, industry, and state funds.	1940: National Defense Research Council established. 1941: Federal Office of Scientific Research and Development established, which contracted for R&D. 1941-1945: Federal laboratories supported war effort for World War II. 1945: Publication of *Science—The Endless Frontier.* 1946-1950: Many federal agencies began funding large amounts of research in universities.	1950: National Science Foundation (NSF) established. 1957-present: Launch of Sputnik catalyzes greater funding of university research. 1957: President's Science Advisory Council and position of presidential advisor for science began. Both were abolished in 1973. 1973: NSF's Industry/ University Cooperative Research Program established. 1974: Office of Science and Technology Policy (OSTP) established in the Executive Office of the President; Director of OSTP named as president's science advisor.	1976: NSF funds research on effects of S&T on local, state, national, and international economies. 1978: NSF begins to support state S&T councils. 1979: NSF establishes Experimental Program to Stimulate Competitive Research (EPSCoR) for states with low levels of research support. 1980: Bayh-Dole Act assigns intellectual property rights for university research to universities.

formerly dean of engineering at the Massachusetts Institute of Technology (MIT) and at that time president of the Carnegie Institution of Washington. Its membership also included the presidents of MIT and Harvard and the president of Bell Laboratories, who at that time was also the president of the National Academy of Sciences. In 1941 the federal government established the Office of Scientific Research and Development (OSRD) in the Executive Office of the President. OSRD, also chaired by Bush, had much more authority than the NDRC—for example, it was able to contract for research and development for military purposes.

The federal government sponsored much more research during World War II than it ever had before, and much of this research either occurred at or was managed by universities. Atomic research that led directly to the Manhattan Project was done at the University of Chicago. The Radiation Laboratory, which developed radar systems, was located on the MIT campus. Research and development at the Los Alamos Laboratory in New Mexico, where the first nuclear weapons were constructed, was managed by the University of California. These wartime research efforts produced remarkable advances, including the atomic bomb, high-frequency radar, sonar cryptography, proximity fuses, and important developments in the medical sciences.

Toward the end of the war, President Roosevelt asked Vannevar Bush to develop a plan, based on the federal government's wartime experiences, to shape the nation's postwar research system. The result was the report *Science—The Endless Frontier*, which was transmitted to President Harry S. Truman on July 5, 1945. In that report, Bush observed that the private sector had the principal responsibility for funding applied research and development. But the market could not guarantee that society would invest sufficiently in basic research because U.S. industry lacked the economic incentive to perform or support research that was widely disseminated in scientific publications. As a result, Bush argued, the federal government should fund basic research as a public good. Furthermore, the report implied that this research should be conducted largely in universities, with the allocation of research funds being determined largely through peer review. It was a plan "unique to the United States," said Atkinson.

Not everything Bush recommended was enacted. He promoted the idea of a national research foundation through which all federal funding for basic research would flow. But resistance from the Congress scuttled that idea, and the National Science Foundation (NSF), which had a more limited mandate, was not established until 1950. In the interim, many other federal agencies, including the Atomic Energy Commission, the National Institutes of Health, the Office of Naval Research, and other parts of the Defense Department, began funding significant amounts of basic research in universities using the peer review process.

The two and a half decades from 1950 until 1975 witnessed "the true flowering of the American research university," said Atkinson. Federal funding of university research increased at a rapid rate, particularly with the launch of Sputnik in 1957. The challenge from the Soviet Union also led President Dwight D. Eisenhower to establish the President's Science Advisory Council (PSAC) and to designate James Killian, president of MIT, as his science advisor. Under the Eisenhower, Kennedy, and to some extent Johnson administrations, PSAC was "central to the workings of government and [had] very high visibility," according to Atkinson. U.S. scientists dominated the ranks of Nobel Prize winners during that period. All of the Nobel prizes in physics from 1950 to 1975 either went to Americans or were shared by Americans. Of the 26 Nobel prizes awarded during that period in chemistry, 18 went to Americans, and Americans received or shared all of the Nobel prizes in medicine or physiology. After the Nobel Prize in economics was established in 1969, six of the first eight winners were Americans. "It was a wonderful period for American science," said Atkinson.

By the end of that period, tensions began to surface. Economic competition from abroad was intensifying, raising the question of whether the university-based research programs of the United States had become too separated from the needs of industry. "There was a feeling that a link between industry and the universities, between basic research and the rest of the chain of research and development, had been broken," said Atkinson. Also, many Americans were becoming restive about the negative influence of new technologies, as the war in Vietnam dragged on and the environmental movement began to take shape. President Lyndon B. Johnson was less happy with PSAC than his predecessors had been "because they were not giving him advice that he thought was very useful in terms of the war," according to Atkinson. Johnson also wanted the scientists on PSAC to help him define his Great Society initiatives to attack poverty and inequality, but PSAC, which consisted largely of physical scientists and mathematicians, "really had nothing to say" about those issues.

When President Richard Nixon was elected in 1968, he was particularly displeased with the scientific community. In his taped conversations, he often spoke with disdain for the research university community, said Atkinson, partly because he felt that the university community in general was opposed to his policies. Funding for research began to taper off during the Nixon years. In 1973, Nixon abolished PSAC and eliminated the position of science advisor.

When he took office after Nixon's 1974 resignation, President Gerald R. Ford, and his vice president, Nelson Rockefeller, were very committed to reinstituting science and technology policy advice in the White House. Working with Congress, they established the Office of Science and Technology Policy (OSTP) in the Executive Office of the President, with the director of OSTP designated as the president's science advisor. At the same time, various federal agencies, private foundations, and professional societies like the National Academy of Sciences began to identify and address some of the shortcomings that had led to tensions in the science and technology system.

One prominent shortcoming was a perceived disconnect between basic research and the marketplace. In response, the National Science Foundation established the Industry/University Cooperative Research Program, which was a "tremendously important program," according to Atkinson (who was NSF director when the program was instituted). Under this program, scientists and engineers in universities worked with their counterparts in industry to submit collaborative proposals to NSF. If the proposal was approved through the peer review process, NSF funded the university side of the project while industry funded work in its laboratories. Although the program initially encountered some resistance, the quality of the proposals was "overwhelming," said Atkinson. "That led to quite a change in funding agencies' approaches to science and technology."

Another response to the gap between universities and industry was the Bayh-Dole Act of 1980. The act assigned the intellectual property rights for research done at universities to the universities themselves, which has meant that the university and individual researchers can profit from their research. In response, universities have set up technology transfer offices to identify and license technologies developed at their institutions. Although these offices are "still not doing the job that needs to be done," said Atkinson, they have helped build connections between university and industry research that had long been neglected.

At that time, NSF also began to fund a program of research into the effects of science and technology on the economy at the state, local, national, and international levels. The result was the development of a body of ideas now known as "new growth theory," which "greatly clarified the powerful role that investments in research play in driving the economy of the country," said Atkinson.

This same period saw the initiation of several additional activities focused on the state level. One was the establishment by NSF in 1979 of the Experimental Program to Stimulate Competitive Research. EPSCoR was designed to ensure that some research funding would flow to states that were disadvantaged in competing with states in which research-intensive universities are located.

Also during this period, NSF helped support and fund state science and technology councils based in part on models at the national level. Although some of these councils have faltered, others have become important players in state policy making (as described later in this report).

Other countries are working hard to emulate the success of the United States in science and technology, including China, Japan, and England. The crucial difference in these countries, according to Atkinson, is that their universities usually are part of national education systems and are overseen by a department or ministry of education. "With all the rules and regulations and constraints, these universities don't have the entrepreneurial character that American universities have had," Atkinson said. "And it's the entrepreneurial character of American universities that has laid the strong foundation for the U.S. science and technology system."

THE FEDERAL LABORATORIES

The laboratories supported by the U.S. Departments of Energy, Defense, Transportation, and Homeland Security; the National Aeronautics and Space Administration; and other federal agencies are another prominent part of the national science and technology system. These laboratories have many different missions, from basic research on the fundamental constituents of matter to the development of military systems. But all can influence science and technology policy advising at the state level, according to Lynn Peters, a vice president with Battelle and former director of the Pacific Northwest National Laboratory, who represented the federal and national laboratories during a panel discussion. "They thrive within their local communities and have an intimate interest [in those communities]," Peters said.

Peters focused on the largest component of the federal laboratories— the national laboratories supported by the Department of Energy (see Figure 2-1).[1] Regional interactions are an integral part of the missions of these laboratories, according to Peters. For example, the Pacific Northwest National Laboratory has worked closely with researchers at the University of Washington and Washington State University to advocate for a Life Sciences Discovery Fund in the state—indeed, one of the laboratory's scientists was the science advisor to a former governor of Washington. "In many ways, we could speak for academia better than they could speak for themselves," said Peters. "We were not the laboratory that was going to get a whole lot of funding out of that $350 million program. But we would be building the science base."

---

[1]A master list of federally funded R&D centers is maintained by the National Science Foundation and is available at http://www.nsf.gov/statistics/nsf06316/ [accessed March 2008].

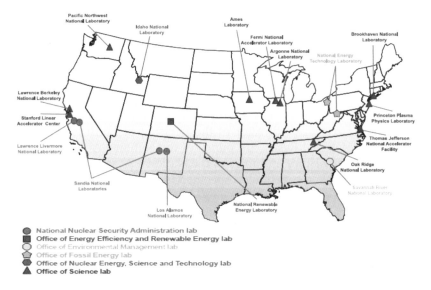

FIGURE 2-1 The U.S. national laboratories.
SOURCE: U.S. Department of Energy.

Similarly, Sandia National Laboratories in New Mexico has participated in the development of a successful science and technology park where businesses work to convert new research into commercial products. Oak Ridge National Laboratory in Tennessee has partnered with the state to form the Joint Institute for Computational Sciences, which is working to develop high-performance computing and communications. And the Department of Homeland Security has worked with the national laboratories to help fulfill its missions. For example, radiation monitors based on research carried out at the national laboratories have been deployed at the nation's borders to detect movements of radioactive materials.

A critical mission for the laboratories in the future, said Peters, will be mitigating climate change. Stabilizing carbon dioxide in the atmosphere at twice the preindustrial level will require a mix of energy sources very different from those of today. Carbon from fossil fuels may be captured and sequestered. And new nuclear power plants will almost certainly need to be built, which will have tremendous implications for state and local policy makers. Yet very little discussion of nuclear power is occurring, Peters pointed out. "We have to look at [nuclear power], and we have to move [the discussion] forward."

THE NATIONAL ACADEMIES

The National Academies are another important institution in the science and technology policy advising system. The National Academy of Sciences, established in 1863 at the request of President Abraham Lincoln under a congressional charter, has had two main functions. One is to honor the nation's top scientists. "It's truly a high honor to be elected, and there are a number of Academy members here in this room," said Warren Muir, executive director of the Division of Earth and Life Sciences at the National Research Council of the National Academies, who summarized the history and roles of the National Academies at the convocation. The second function, as specified in the Academy's charter, has been, "whenever called upon by any department of the Government, [to] investigate, examine, experiment, and report upon any subject of science or art."[2] In this capacity, the institution has functioned as an advisor to the federal government for many years, and its reports often have influenced other levels of government (including individual states) and private organizations.

Today the National Academies consist of four entities: the National Academy of Sciences, the National Academy of Engineering, the Institute of Medicine, and the National Research Council. Like the National Academy of Sciences, the National Academy of Engineering and Institute of Medicine are honorific. They were established in 1964 and 1970, respectively, to honor the nation's top engineers, medical researchers, and physicians and also to provide policy advice to the government.

The National Research Council (NRC) was established in 1916 as a way to expand the range of expertise involved in policy deliberations beyond the membership of the National Academy of Sciences. Committees of experts organized under the National Research Council release more than 250 reports each year on a wide variety of topics, from the safety and security of spent nuclear fuel, to guidelines for human embryonic stem cell research, to the ecological impacts of climate change, to national standards for science education in grades K-12. Committees are carefully vetted, and committee members disclose any potential conflicts of interest with the subject being addressed. "Each person discusses their expertise and perspectives on the issues so that we make sure that we have the right expertise and the right balance of perspectives," said Muir. In some cases, committees are adjusted as a study proceeds to add expertise or achieve a better balance of perspectives. Draft reports from committees are reviewed by experts who are not on the committee and by representatives of the NRC and are revised as needed before being

---

[2]"Art" at the time the charter was instituted was synonymous with "technology" today.

made public. All of the reports are publicly available except for a small fraction on classified subjects, and for these reports a public summary of the report is available.[3]

The studies can be expensive, often costing hundreds of thousands of dollars to cover staff time and to convene committees. Reports often take a year or more to complete, although some have been done in much less time when a project calls for a quick response.

The National Academies have always been separate from and independent of the federal government—operating as a 501C(3) organization—and the members of committees serve without compensation. The National Academies are not an advocacy organization or a consultant for the private sector. With a few exceptions, Academies reports analyze and synthesize already existing information and evidence and are produced in response to requests from government agencies or nongovernmental organizations. "The Academy is a service entity," said Muir. "We take on the questions that people come to us with and that are funded."

Among the National Academies' strengths are "the organization's unique credibility and its unparalleled ability to draw in the best experts from around the country, and indeed from around the world," Muir said. Because the National Academies are not an advocacy or a stakeholder organization, they are highly valued for their independence. However, the National Academies also lack the capacity in general to follow up once a project is complete. When a report is issued, the authoring committee usually disbands and the institution moves on to new projects. As a result, said Muir, the institution cannot "interpret and follow through with legislators or others on most of our reports."

The organizations that make up the National Academies are national in scope, but they often examine issues that have important implications at the state and local levels. NRC committees have looked at such diverse issues as the introduction of foreign oysters into the Chesapeake Bay, the Louisiana coastal protection restoration program, and the safety of a proposed biosafety facility to be built in Boston. Committees also work with state organizations, such as universities or state academies of science.

The federal government funds most studies conducted by the National Academies, but funding also comes from many other sources, including the states. In some cases, states also appeal to federal agencies or to their congressional representatives to fund a study of special relevance to that state. Sponsors cannot see the reports as they are being written and reviewed because the National Academies are exempt by an act of Congress from the requirements of the Federal Advisory Committee Act

---

[3]Electronic versions of all 4,000+ National Academies reports are available at <http://www.nap.edu>.

(FACA).[4] As a result, sponsors "don't know what they are going to get," said Muir. "They end up receiving the report once it is final."

A CASE STUDY: MANAGING THE COLUMBIA RIVER BASIN

In his talk, Gerry O'Keefe, Columbia River policy coordinator of the Washington State Department of Ecology, provided an excellent example of how the NRC works with states when he spoke about an NRC committee that focused on an issue of direct relevance for Washington State.

The Columbia River carries 200 million acre-feet of water in an average year, (which, coincidentally, is about the same size as the water budget for the state of California, O'Keefe noted). It drains an area of 273,000 square miles that extends from Canada to Wyoming and Utah. It is a tightly controlled system that is managed for flood control, for agriculture, for power generation, and for protection of the salmon that live and spawn in the river.

Factors affecting the river are undergoing profound changes, O'Keefe pointed out. Population growth is increasing the demands being made of the river. Climate change, particularly as it affects mountain snowpacks, could alter the amount of water that the river can supply. Salmon species in the river are in decline, even though salmon have an "iconic value" to the people of Washington State. And the river continues to offer untapped potential for economic development. According to one calculation, withdrawing 1 million acre-feet of water, which is about half of 1 percent of the annual flow of the Columbia, and applying it to the land would create 18,000 jobs and annual revenues of approximately $850 million. "This is a number that is not ever ignored by the governor's office" or the state legislature, said O'Keefe. "It captures and crystallizes their attention like almost nothing else will."

For decades, the state has struggled to develop policies to manage the Columbia River Basin. Many groups have conflicting interests in the Columbia River, including farmers, other private interests, the federal government, the environmental community, and 13 Indian tribes that rely on the river's water. As discussions among these groups deteriorated over the years, management decisions became increasingly difficult. "You were either on one side or you were on the other, and there was no middle ground," said O'Keefe. When state officials or others in charge of mediating among the sides tried to arrange meetings, the sides would not even agree to talk unless they knew what the outcome of the discussion was likely to be. Different groups "have veto power," said O'Keefe. "The

---

[4]For more information about the Federal Advisory Committee Act, see <http://www.gsa.gov/Portal/gsa/ep/contentView.do?contentType=GSA_BASIC&contentId=11635>.

federal statute is designed with overlapping authorities and jurisdictions, and unless you have something close to consensus, you're going to find out that you're unable to act."

Washington State had decided that it could not rely totally on local sources of advice for decisions about managing the river. Experts in the state who were qualified to offer advice had mostly worked on specific aspects of the problem previously. These individuals probably could and would have done their best work, said O'Keefe, but they were compromised by their proximity to the issue. "We needed policy innovation, we needed policy consensus," said O'Keefe. "We needed something to cut through the gridlock."

In 2002 the state turned to the Water Science and Technology Board at the NRC for help. The first task was to define the question to be answered. "We spent a tremendous amount of time and energy thinking about what it was we were going to ask the National Academy of Sciences to resolve for us." The actual charge covered most of two pages, but it can be boiled down to a relatively simple question, according to O'Keefe: "If 1 million acre-feet of water were to be removed from the river, what impact would that action have on endangered species, and what could be done to mitigate those impacts?"

The state did not know what the response from the NRC committee would be, and the final report from the Water Science and Technology Board (National Research Council, 2004) did not deliver the answer that the state expected, according to O'Keefe. State officials expected that a relatively small withdrawal of water from the river was unlikely to have a measurable effect on the salmon. The NRC report said otherwise. It said that salmon populations were in trouble, especially during the summer when the flow of the river is lower and the water is warmer. The conclusion of the report, said O'Keefe, was that "you need to be very careful as you allocate water out of the stream. You are getting yourself into a situation where you could end up with a year or a series of years where you have lost your management flexibility and you have in fact predetermined that you will lose your species as well."

Once the report was delivered, policy makers in Washington State had to decide what to do with the NRC's advice. This was not a foregone conclusion, said O'Keefe. State legislators "really are representative of the communities that elect them. They come from all kinds of backgrounds. . . . Our challenge is to try to find ways to . . . connect with those people who have the ability to make those decisions." To their credit, despite the many pressures exerted on them, the state's policy makers did not ignore the advice. "We tried, to the extent we could, to be guided by the National Academies to create a flexible and responsive policy framework on the fly that helped us break through the policy gridlock that we had experienced as a state." The state opted to look at additional storage developments for Columbia River water and at the use of existing storage facilities. Of every three quantities of water made newly available through this process, one would be set aside for protection of the salmon. "We linked the economic interest of the state to the long-term environmental interest of the state in a way that I think is really quite creative, and it turned out to be quite compelling and powerful," O'Keefe said. Legislation authorizing the creation of a new water program was supported with $200 million of funding to develop water supplies over time. And conversations with Canada and with surrounding states were initiated to manage the river more effectively. "The future in Washington State as a result of this conversation is really quite a lot brighter," O'Keefe concluded.

3

The Current Landscape for State Science and Technology Policy Advice

The states already have an extensive and expanding array of activities that have direct links to science and technology. Many of these activities were summarized in the report *Investing in Innovation*, which was supported by the Pew Center on the States (2007)[1] as part of a larger initiative on innovation led by the National Governors Association.[2] At the convocation, Doug Henton summarized the findings from *Investing in Innovation* and pointed to some of the report's implications.

An increasing number of states are funding research directly, Henton observed. Some states, including California, Iowa, New York, and Texas, have been especially aggressive. The 2004 passage of Proposition 71 in California set aside up to $3 billion for stem cell research. California is also investing $400 million in its Institutes of Science and Innovation: under the initiative the campuses in the University of California system are working on critical issues like climate change, energy, and traffic congestion; private universities, including Stanford, the University of Southern California, and the California Institute of Technology, are also participating in this initiative.

Other states not typically known for their commitments to research are making substantial investments in science and technology, including Arizona, Colorado, Florida, Indiana, North Dakota, Ohio, Oklahoma,

---

[1]For additional information about the Pew Center on the States, see <http://www.pewcenteronthestates.org>.

[2]For additional information about the National Governors Association, see <http://nga.org>.

Virginia, Washington State, and West Virginia. Oklahoma has established the Oklahoma Center for Advanced Science and Technology.[3] Washington State has set aside $350 million for a Life Sciences Discovery Fund.[4] North Dakota has established Centers of Excellence[5] focused on issues like water quality and the environment. "They're getting into the game and doing it well," said Henton.

States have funded these efforts in a variety of ways. Sometimes they have earmarked increased tax revenues approved by popular votes or by state legislatures. For example, the people of Arizona approved a sales tax increase that will generate $1 billion over 20 years to be distributed among three public universities to expand funding for research, technology transfer, and new business development. The West Virginia legislature set aside 0.5 percent of the state's racetrack lottery proceeds, which was $4 million per year in 2005 and 2006, to fund research and development at institutions of higher learning, increase competitiveness for external funding, and support science and mathematics education programs. Some states have set aside funds from general appropriations. The Georgia Research Alliance uses part of its $30 million in annual public and private funding to recruit eminent scholars to Georgia universities,[6] and Kentucky's "Bucks for Brains" initiative has invested about $350 million in state funds for similar purposes.[7] Washington State's Life Sciences Discovery Fund is using money from the state's settlement with tobacco companies, and Kansas is setting aside tax revenue that exceeds a base year amount for the Kansas Bioscience Authority.[8]

Many of these initiatives seek to take advantage of the physical proximity of researchers, businesses, and policy makers. Even in the age of the Internet, said Henton, "the most creative work is still face to face. Routine work can be done elsewhere. Having people together and interacting and thinking together is still very valuable." For example, Pennsylvania has supported a Keystone Innovation Zone,[9] where researchers from Carnegie

---

[3]For additional information about the Oklahoma Center for Advanced Science and Technology, see <http://www.ocast.state.ok.us>.

[4]For additional information about the State of Washington's Life Sciences Discovery Fund, see <http://www.lsdfa.org/home.html>.

[5]For additional information about North Dakota's Centers of Excellence, see <http://governor.state.nd.us/media/speeches/040325.html>.

[6]For additional information about the Georgia Research Alliance, see <http://www.gra.org/eminentscholars.asp>.

[7]For additional information about Kentucky's "Bucks for Brains" initiative, see <http://www.research.uky.edu/students/rctf.html>.

[8]For additional information about the Kansas Bioscience Authority, see <http://www.kansasbioauthority.org>.

[9]For additional information about Pennsylvania's Keystone Innovation Zone, see <http://www.lehighvalley.org/page.cfm?pag=477>.

Mellon University and the University of Pittsburgh work together with the industry. In the Torrey Pines area north of San Diego, the Scripps Research Institute, the Salk Institute, and the University of California, San Diego, are all within a few miles of each other, which has helped make the area as active in biotechnology as San Francisco and Boston. "Everything is within walking distance," said Henton. "That means heads get together and can do more collaboration."

Proximity is also an important factor for financing. "What I've learned from friends in Silicon Valley is that venture capital is a contact sport," said Henton. The University of California has encouraged university professors to get involved with industry, which can lead to spinoff companies, and the Bay Area Science and Engineering Consortium[10] is doing good work, according to Henton.

In general, the states are not trying to fund everything. The states use their funding "for leverage," said Henton. "They put money in to connect the federal dollars and the industry dollars through these various centers. They use it for bridging gaps. . . . The federal government was not there [for stem cell research in California], and the state decided it wanted to fill that gap. Maybe clean energy fits into that right now."

State funding also tends to be focused on commercialization. Several speakers at the convocation mentioned the "valley of death," where good ideas generated by researchers languish and eventually expire before they are developed enough to yield commercial products. State funding can help new products and services get through the valley of death, by making connections between researchers and innovators. The federal government excels in mission-oriented funding, like building a particular weapon system, attacking a human disease, or cleaning up a waste site. "But they're not so good at commercialization," said Henton. "That's not their purpose." Because of the close ties between state governments and industries in those states, state funding for research can help develop an "innovation habit," Henton said, which can hasten the commercialization process.

STATE AGENCIES

In each state government, specific agencies often are a focus of policy and decision making that involves science and technology. At the convocation, Larry McKinney, director of coastal fisheries for the Texas Parks and Wildlife Department, described some of the issues in developing science-based natural resource policies as part of a regulatory process.

---

[10]For additional information about California's Bay Area Science and Engineering Consortium, see <http://www.bayareabiotechnology.com/resourcecenter/directory.htm>.

A major challenge, said McKinney, is that the variability of natural systems can mask the effects of pollution, overexploitation of resources, or climate change. Opponents of a particular policy can then point to natural variability or other aspects of natural systems as evidence of flaws in the science base supporting a policy, which can complicate or stymie the development of clear and convincing support for policy recommendations. Opponents of a policy also can advocate continued study of an issue to be as certain as possible about a decision. In effect, this can be a delaying tactic, even when it is advocated with the best of intentions.

A source of friction between science and technology advisors and policy makers is the basis on which they evaluate options, McKinney observed. Policy makers often bring socioeconomic and political considerations to bear on a decision. What may appear to be the obvious decision to scientists or engineers based on a logical analysis may not be (and often is not) as obvious to policy makers, who look at issues from a very different perspective. They key for policy advisors is to understand that there are other valuation systems that are not necessarily wrong—they're just different. "If there is to be any real hope for long-term success," Kinney pointed out, "science-based policy making must take people into account."

McKinney pointed toward the value of adaptive management, in which the effects of a management decision are continually assessed to evaluate the outcomes of the decision. If applied honestly and rigorously, adaptive management can yield meaningful progress while leaving open the opportunity to make corrections when new information becomes available. In addition, data from long-term environmental monitoring can be a powerful and confidence-building tool for both advisors and policy makers.

STATE SCIENCE ADVISORS

Across the states, some governors choose to appoint science advisors, and others do not. Also, the appointment of a science advisor by one governor does not necessarily mean that his or her successor in the office will retain that advisor or even the position of advisor. As a result, the presence of a single person to provide science and technology policy advice in an official capacity in state governments varies from state to state and over time.

Yet science advisors can have an influence that cannot be achieved in other ways, said Tom Bowles, who has been science advisor to New Mexico Governor Bill Richardson since 2006. Bowles, a nuclear physicist who worked at Los Alamos National Laboratory for more than two decades before becoming the governor's science advisor, used his own experience in New Mexico to describe the role of state science advisors.

New Mexico is "a land of contrasts," Bowles said. The state has the highest numbers of Ph.D.s per capita of any state and some of the poorest counties in the nation. New Mexico also is "a land of science," he said. It has the highest R&D funding per capita of any state, largely because of the presence of two large national laboratories there. Together, Los Alamos and Sandia national laboratories employ more than 20,000 people, including more than 8,000 Ph.D. researchers. Along with the Air Force Research Laboratory at Kirkland Air Force Base, the White Sands Missile Base, and researchers at the state's colleges and universities, the state has a strong base of highly trained scientists and engineers.

In a state in which science is so prominent, having a science advisor is critical, said Bowles. For example, with the exception of Intel, New Mexico does not have large high-technology companies. Bowles has therefore focused considerable attention on using the resources of the national laboratories and universities for high-tech economic development. "It's an area where we have tremendous potential. To be honest, we have not done that well in the past. Laboratories, especially the defense labs, have been pretty much behind the fence. We're trying to change that."

Bowles cited as an example a computing applications center initiative that he helped develop. The initiative called for the development of a premier high-performance computing center in New Mexico that is directed at applications, not basic research. Governor Richardson made it a high priority, and the state has decided to put $42 million into what will be a $300 million investment over five years. The center will have a permanent staff of about 60 and 200 visiting staff, including a large number of students.

It has adopted a structure different from that of other computing centers around the country, based on partnerships with local companies or local branches of national and international companies, so that interactions are on a face-to-face basis. It is also going to have a strong educational component, with K-12 students involved in the collaborations. "That's really important because most of our K-12 students never are on a college campus when they're deciding whether or not they want to go to college," said Bowles. "The same thing with businesses. Get them connected with the students, and vice versa. Let the students see some of the exciting opportunities so that they'll stay, finish their degrees, and work there."

In New Mexico, the role of the science advisor is more than one of just providing advice. Bowles has been involved in shaping policies, forming initiatives, and leading those initiatives to be implemented. He also emphasized how important it is for a science advisor simply to be present.

"If you have a science advisor sitting in the governor's office, you have a person who is hearing everything that's going on all the time, not just in science, but in transportation and homeland security and health and education and everything else. And where appropriate, you can jump in and say, 'Wait a minute, science ought to have some say in this. There is a solution. There are some options here. We have a way to help you.'" Because science and technology advisory groups are often responding to specific requests, they have more difficulty in identifying situations that seem not to directly involve science and technology but where they can be helpful.

Furthermore, someone with a technical background can have a huge impact at the state level, said Bowles, because "my experience has been [that] most state agencies are so consumed with the process of just doing business, they never are in a position to lay out what the long-term issues of importance for the state are." For example, the governor recently asked Bowles to put together an energy roadmap for the state given a carbon-constrained economy. A recent three-day meeting brought together national leaders, economists, engineers, utility managers, environmentalists, citizen groups, water resource managers, and others to look at not only coal, oil, and gas but also wind power, new transmission lines, geothermal energy, and biomass. Having such wide representation is particularly helpful in identifying contradictions in plans, Bowles said. For example, plans to grow biomass to serve as transportation fuels require large quantities of water, but water supplies are very tight in arid states like New Mexico.

COLLEGES AND UNIVERSITIES

As several speakers at the convocation noted, colleges and universities can have a critical influence on state science and technology policies. At the most general level, institutions of higher education help create the human resources and innovation climate that drive technological, economic, and policy progress. "How universities impact public policy is through the creation of intellectual capital, and in today's society, intellectual capital is business capital," said Holly Harris Bane, associate vice president for strategic initiatives and engagement at the University of Akron in Ohio. "Universities serve as an engine for the creation, distribution, and application of knowledge."

State governments also can forge close partnerships with colleges and universities through both budgeting and governance. In turn, researchers at colleges and universities can provide state policy and decision makers with the scientific and technical information they need to do their jobs. For example, the University of California system serves as a research organization for the entire state, Doug Henton pointed out, and universities in other states also play that role.

As institutions of higher education assume a larger role in the economic development of their states, the economic and policy impact of colleges and universities other than the major research universities has been growing. For example, the regional comprehensive universities are becoming "more directly oriented toward the mission and structure of applied research and development," said Robert McMahan, science and technology advisor for the state of North Carolina. According to McMahan, funding directed specifically toward mission-oriented and applied research at these institutions can be especially effective at spurring the development of local economies.

STATE ACADEMIES OF SCIENCE

Other valuable resources are the state academies of science that exist in more than 40 states. These academies can be very different kinds of institutions, ranging from consortia of museums to honorific societies to providers of scientific information for their state governments, and some are much stronger or more active than others. Currently, many are not much involved in policy decisions, but they have great potential to do more. As Ed Haddad, executive director of the Florida Academy of Sciences, said, "I wish that more state legislators and gubernatorial offices knew that there are state academies of science in their state because we're a terrific resource."

Lynn Elfner, the chief executive officer of the Ohio Academy of Science and a member of the convocation planning group, described the role of academies in depth at the convocation. The functions of state academies of science and engineering, which can trace their origins to Plato's school of philosophy at Akademia, include archiving knowledge, providing a venue for the presentation of original research, fostering education in science and mathematics, engaging in public outreach, and to some extent provide science and technology policy advice to state governments. Representatives of the state academies meet each year at the annual meeting of the National Association of Academies of Science,[11] which was founded in 1926 and is an affiliate of the American Association for the Advancement of Science.

An area of expertise of many state academies is agriculture, said Elfner. The Ohio Academy of Science, for example, was founded in 1891

---

[11]For links to the websites of individual state academies of science and engineering, visit the website of the National Association of Academies of Science, see <http://astro.physics.sc.edu/NAAS>.

by members of the Ohio Agricultural Research and Development Center.[12] "Things like pest management, control of diseases, and soils are a very strong forte of the state academies, [along with] broader issues of crop productivity," said Elfner. "One of the world's experts on soybeans is a member of the Ohio Academy of Science, for example."

Another area of strength is natural resource policy, such as water policies or the use of coal or other mineral resources. Many state academies have members who have inventoried these resources and know them well. For example, most state geologists are members of their state academies. Studies of the environment, water quality, or endangered species often are published in academy-sponsored journals. The *Ohio Journal of Science*,[13] for example, often publishes studies that provide benchmark data for environmental issues important to the state. The Ohio Academy of Science also has provided state policy makers with a list of experts on energy policy, several of whom have testified before the Ohio General Assembly.

State academies can influence state science and technology policy in two major ways, according to Elfner. First, they can inform the budget process, especially when a new governor is coming into office and reshaping the budget to reflect new priorities. "Getting involved in the budget process, knowing the sequence of the process and understanding the pinch points, so to speak, is where you can really make a difference," he said.

Second, state academies can influence regulatory issues and the adoption of standards for education, water quality, land use, and so on. Most state academies have members who are officials in state agencies, or they have members who can give advice to boards, commissions, or task forces. For example, a task force in Ohio recently examined environmental problems involving Lake Erie, and about half of the members of the task force were academy members. In these ways, state academies can provide "the technical advice to ensure that standards are reasonable and have some basis in science," Elfner said.

> *Getting involved in the budget process, knowing the sequence of the process and understanding the pinch points, so to speak, is where you can really make a difference.*

---

[12]For additional information about the Ohio Agricultural Research and Development Center, see <http://www.oardc.ohio-state.edu>.

[13]For additional information about the *Ohio Journal of Science*, see <http://www.ohiosci.org/ojs.htm>.

State academies also can play a prominent role in science, technology, engineering, and mathematics education, both by influencing state education standards and funding and by supporting individual students. Many future science and engineering leaders presented papers or projects at state academies when they were high school or college students. For example, George Rieveschl, the inventor of Benadryl®, gave his first technical paper in 1937 as an undergraduate at a meeting of the Ohio Academy of Science. "I could go on and on [naming] numerous others who made their first entry into the scientific community through a state academy of science," said Elfner.

State academies also can monitor the policy process. For example, challenges to the teaching of evolution in public schools can be tracked and confronted by the members of state academies, with assistance from national organizations like the National Academy of Sciences.

Many state academies are small and do not have permanent staffs. They also are not necessarily politically savvy, since members of the academies may be largely separated from the political process. Some academies may be able to monitor legislative actions, but others do not or cannot do so. For the same reason, they may not be able to mount a rapid response when the need arises.

Despite these limitations, state academies can be particularly adept at putting together coalitions of state organizations to advocate for particular policies. Sometimes they also can work through national organizations that have local chapters, like Sigma Xi[14] or professional associations. For example, the director of the Ohio Society of Professional Engineers is a senator in the state. Sigma Xi, in particular, is active in many communities and is multidisciplinary, so it can address many different topics. Sigma Xi "has a chapter structure that lends itself well to being utilized at state, local, and regional levels," said Kelly Sullivan, director of institutional partnerships for Pacific Northwest National Laboratory.

STATE SCIENCE AND TECHNOLOGY COUNCILS

Several states have organizations made up of scientists and engineers that serve functions similar to those of the National Research Council. One of the most prominent is the California Council on Science and Technology (CCST), which was described at the convocation by its executive director Susan Hackwood.

The CCST was formed about 20 years ago and was modeled explicitly on the National Research Council. It has 30 members, split more or less evenly between academia and business, and includes many of the state's

---

[14]For additional information about Sigma Xi, see <http://www.sigmaxi.org>.

science and technology leaders. In addition, the CCST has some 150 appointed fellows, who provide a rich source of expertise for conducting studies. The major federal laboratories in the state, along with the Department of Energy and the National Aeronautics and Space Administration, are affiliated with the council.

The CCST is funded by state agencies, foundations, and industries. It receives core funding from the three public systems of higher education and three leading private universities in the state, and that core funding is critical, according to Hackwood. "Over the years, it has enabled us to live through the changes that occur so rapidly at that state level." Like the NRC, the CCST has processes for council members to disclose potential conflicts of interest and submit draft reports to peer review.[15] It also seeks to expedite the production of its reports so that state legislators can receive findings when the information is most useful.

The council focuses on topics requested by the state, but it also takes on projects that it thinks are important even without a specific request. As a result, it maintains its impartiality, which is "extremely important," according to Hackwood. Also, the CCST often arrives at conclusions "that may not be exactly the solution that people are looking for," Hackwood said.

Recent projects undertaken by the CCST have focused on nanotechnology, intellectual property, biotechnology, genetically engineered foods, energy, climate change, health care information, the preparation of science and mathematics teachers, masters-level science education, and state competitiveness. For example, the CCST recently conducted an independent review of a $62.5 million energy research project in the state that was initiated after deregulation of the energy industry in the 1990s. A 2004 interim report drew attention to management deficiencies in the program. "This caused substantive changes within the management structure of the Energy Commission," Hackwood said, so that when the final report came out in 2005, its recommendations had already been implemented.

When the National Academies report *Rising Above the Gathering Storm: Energizing and Employing America for a Brighter Economic Future* was released in 2005,[16] the governor of California asked the CCST to translate the report's recommendations to the state level. Four separate task groups led by industry leaders extracted from the report the messages most relevant to California, which led specifically to several important educational initiatives at the state level, according to Hackwood.

---

[15]For more information about the NRC's policies on bias and conflict of interest, see <http://www.nationalacademies.org/coi/index.html>.

[16]This report was updated in 2007 (see National Academy of Sciences, National Academy of Engineering, and Institute of Medicine, 2007).

Sometimes the CCST considers itself successful when something does *not* happen. For example, a study of genetically modified foods helped keep labels from being placed on school lunch foods in a way not justified by the existing scientific evidence. Similarly, the study of nanotechnology told state legislators that nanotechnology was going to be neither an economic savior nor an environmental peril. And because of term limits in California, the council has found that in some cases it has to make arguments repeatedly for new legislators.

The CCST has held a series of joint meetings with the National Academies. For example, a fall 2006 meeting with the National Academy of Engineering[17] examined the future of sustainable energy in the state and developed a process for informing the state legislature and administration on opportunities for future energy resources. That effort led to a request from the lieutenant governor to look at the future of nuclear energy in California. The council is also looking at the effects of climate change on the state. The emphasis has been examining "climate change in my backyard," said Hackwood. "What happens to me in the next five to ten years is going to affect the way that I do business, the way that I purchase land, the way that I make decisions, [such as whether] to put air conditioning in San Francisco, which the city has never needed before." The council also is looking at the effects of climate change on transportation, the California coast, land acquisition, and the stewardship of public funds.

Several years ago, the National Academies formed a Teacher Advisory Council (TAC),[18] and CCST has similarly formed a California Teachers Advisory Council (CalTAC).[19] CalTAC consists of a group of practicing science and mathematics teachers who advise the CSST on all aspects of its education work. "If we don't pay attention to what's going on with K-12 education, we're not going to have much of a future in terms of our growth of science and engineering," Hackwood said. The TAC and CalTAC have collaborated to examine the professional development of science and mathematics teachers as well as several related topics (e.g., National Research Council, 2007). Not all of the council's recommendations have been accepted. For example, it has recommended that the governor appoint a science and technology advisor, which has not yet happened. "Bringing this kind of expertise to assist the state is really a challenge," Hackwood said. "It sometimes works, and it sometimes doesn't."

---

[17]For more information about the National Academy of Engineering, see <http://nae.edu>.

[18]For more information about the National Academies Teacher Advisory Council, see <http://www7.nationalacademies.org/tac>.

[19]For additional information about the California Teacher Advisory Council, see <http://www.ccst.us/ccstinfo/caltac.php>.

4

Institutional Structures for Enhancing State Science and Technology Policy Advice

Most of the institutional structures needed to greatly improve state-level science and technology policy advice already exist. The challenge is to adapt and coordinate these institutions to meet the needs of states and to take advantage of the many opportunities that are currently available.

COLLEGES AND UNIVERSITIES

Holly Harris Bane described the many ways in which colleges and universities can provide science and technology policy advice to state officials. Colleges and universities—in addition to educating students and creating new knowledge—can directly provide state policy and decision makers with information. This may require frequent and repeated interactions with state legislators, especially in states where term limits continually bring new cohorts of lawmakers to state capitals, as mentioned earlier. These state legislators "are bright individuals in many, many ways," said Bane. "They wouldn't be where they are [otherwise]. But they're put into a situation—and often within two years into significant leadership roles— where they have to be making policy decisions that truly impact us."

One important lesson for university researchers who are interacting with state legislators is to focus on problems that need to be solved. The work that faculty members are doing may be interesting, but to be useful state legislators must be able to do something with the information they get from researchers. "That may seem obvious," Bane said, "but it's not always obvious to our faculty members."

> *One important lesson for university researchers who are interacting with state legislators is to focus on problems that need to be solved. The work that faculty members are doing may be interesting, but to be useful state legislators must be able to do something with the information they get from researchers.*

Bane recommends that when faculty members are preparing to testify or meet with state legislators, they seek to make their message concise— just a half minute or a minute. "You have to have data to back it up, but the first time you have access to an elected official, you don't pull out all the data," Bane said. "Once you get the hook, then you have all the data-driven information behind it."

Bane also pays close attention to the political currents at the local, state, and federal levels. "The world is political in terms of influencing public policy, and [it] definitely helps when all the political stars are aligned." Proponents of change need to try to align the political forces to move a policy ahead.

Partly for that reason, university outreach to legislators is generally most effective when it is done in partnership with other institutions. Bane said that progress has been especially notable when the university has partnered with other colleges and universities, with professional societies, and with businesses. In particular, "our best success in terms of influencing public policy has been when industry has been able to step up and get involved in the process." The individuals who are willing to champion an issue often come from the private sector, Bane noted, and these champions are more likely to be risk takers. Such commitments and innovations are often necessary to move an initiative forward.

Colleges and universities also should focus on systemic change rather than one-time commitments. Sometimes this requires broadening the focus of an initiative to include the interests of multiple stakeholders. For example, a policy initiative focused largely on homeland security made little progress in Ohio until the initiative was broadened to include an economic development theme. Another example is a science and mathematics education initiative that languished until it was broadened to include instruction in "critical languages" that are important to U.S. interests.

Finally, colleges and universities have a direct impact on K-12 education through the teachers and administrators they educate, and the importance of K-12 education to the prospects of individual states and the nation as a whole cannot be overstated. The success of innovation at the state level is "contingent upon a successful public K-12 educational system," said Karl Pister. "We must never forget that. This is a systems problem in the most elaborate sense of the word 'system.'"

> *The success of innovation at the state level is contingent upon a successful public K-12 educational system. We must never forget that. This is a systems problem in the most elaborate sense of the word "system."*

Despite the importance of colleges and universities, there is serious concern about the "systemic structural issues associated with sustaining the university structures that are necessary for supporting economic innovation," said M.R.C. Greenwood, former provost and senior vice president for academic affairs for the University of California. The United States is spending a smaller percentage of its gross domestic product on publicly funded research and development than are other countries, despite calls in national reports, such as *Rising Above the Gathering Storm*, to boost the U.S. research and development system, and this funding shortfall needs to be a focus of policy makers' attention, she observed.

STATE ACADEMIES AND COUNCILS

The more than 40 state academies of science in the United States have great potential to offer science and technology policy advice, but today that potential is largely untapped. The members of state academies have a tendency to "talk to each other, not to other people," said Charles Lytle, president of the North Carolina Academy of Sciences. According to Ed Haddad, "The state academies are not always recognized for the expertise that they do contain and are not utilized enough as a resource," even though state academies are often thoroughly aware of the issues being dealt with at the state level. Larry McKinney cited the same experience in Texas: "We have many resources, but they're not used by our legislature."

In seeking to influence state policies involving science and technology, academies need to reach out not only to state legislators and governors but also to the business communities in each state, said John Burch of the Kansas firm Ergosyst Associates. Many businesses are not aware of the resources that a state academy can offer, even when their business is based on science and technology.

Many of the state academies have common interests and opportunities. For this reason, they could learn a great deal from each other. Several people at the convocation suggested that the state academies work together specifically to coordinate their efforts and share best practices, perhaps under the auspices of an organization like the National Academy of Sciences or the American Association for the Advancement of Science. The involvement of a national organization also could help state academies attract the interest of younger researchers.

State academies have many options in seeking to influence state science and technology policy (many of these options are discussed in the next chapter "Communicating Science and Technology Policy Advice Effectively"). For example, Haddad described an initiative undertaken after the Florida Academy of Sciences arranged to have two scientists speak on a television show called the "Daily Buzz" that is widely broadcast in the United States.[1] Since then, the academy has developed a list of proposed small television segments that is being sent to media in the central Florida area.

Such efforts emphasize the importance of being proactive rather than reactive. Researchers need to put their case forward, said Bowles, as businesses, environmental groups, utilities, and many other organizations do. Such involvement often requires special training, which could be provided or supported by such organizations as the National Academies.

Participants also were enthusiastic about the potential for advisory groups, like the California Council on Science and Technology, to influence state policies. These councils can connect policy makers to the science and technology knowledge base in a state, and their independence enables them to provide a perspective that may not be available through other means. It is important, however, that such councils be sustainable if they are to provide independent and timely advice. "If you depend on a state budget, it can go up and down and disappear at any point," said Atkinson.

Atkinson suggested that those who have had experience with state councils of science and technology list the ingredients that make a council effective and enduring. States also could compare their experiences with advisory councils in science and technology to extract lessons about what works and to foster the much more widespread creation and use of such councils. "It's really something that should be done, in my judgment, in every state in the nation," said Atkinson.

STATE SCIENCE AND TECHNOLOGY ADVISORS

A state science and technology advisor can be a particularly powerful influence on state policies, partly because he or she can emphasize the

---

[1]More information about "The Daily Buzz" is available at <http://dailybuzz.tv/>.

pervasive influence of science and technology on policy. Many policy makers tend to view science and technology as a filter on policy—in other words, science and technology are factors in some policies but not others. A science and technology advisor, said McMahon, can demonstrate that science and technology are actually "organizing principles for government and policy." According to Elfner, "the policy arena is much broader than the policy du jour, so to speak. We need to keep in mind that there are mechanisms that need to be in place to affect policy all across the board, in all the fields of science, technology, and engineering."

> *Many policy makers tend to view science and technology as a filter on policy—in other words, science and technology are factors in some policies but not others. A science and technology advisor can demonstrate that science and technology are actually organizing principles for government and policy.*

Tom Bowles laid out what he sees as the desired characteristics of a science advisor. The first quality is to have an advisor who has demonstrated success in leading and managing research and development. "Leadership means you have to be credible," Bowles said. "If people . . . think you are just someone who's a pure academic, who's never done much except table-top research, businesses and large organizations are not going to pay much attention to you." Other people should recognize an advisor's role in making decisions. This may require that science advisors do some self-promoting, and "scientists are not much used to promoting themselves." But science advisors may need to make their credentials and accomplishments more apparent. People should hear that "you have to go talk to this person if you want to get something done."

A second important qualification is breadth of knowledge. "You have to know what you're talking about," said Bowles. This can be difficult for scientists because of the specialization of research. "I remember when I passed my general exams at Princeton, [my faculty advisors] said, 'Congratulations, you now know more science than you will at any other time in your life.' And they were right, because after that you start narrowing down, you know a whole lot more about a little bit." But in today's economy, cross-disciplinary interactions are essential, even though academic researchers tend to specialize in their own fields.

A third qualification is strong communication skills. The people you are advising need to know what you're saying. "I remember the first cabinet meeting I went to with Governor Richardson. I started talking about some of the opportunities in information technology, in nanotechnology, in biotechnology, and at the end, the governor said, 'Tom, that was really great. But half the people in this room don't have a single idea what you just said.' And he then went on to translate it since, as secretary of energy, he had a strong background in [these subjects]. Even though you try and tone it down, it can still be a challenge."

Expressing ideas in relevant terms does not mean "dumbing down" an idea. Rather, it means talking to people in terms they understand. "We're an agricultural state, and I'll tell you, the farmers and ranchers [I meet] are some of the smartest people I know. You can't profit [in farming and ranching] unless you know what you're doing," commented Bowles. Advisors also need to be able to address a very wide range of legislators. "Some of them don't even own a personal computer or have an e-mail address. Some of them are incredibly tech-savvy. Most of them are in the middle. They know it's important, but they can't tell you why and they can't explain it to their constituents. You've got to get through that."

The fourth qualification is the ability to perform. "You can't be all talk. Politics is a hands-on sport. You need to get in and convince the legislature. You need to do things. You need to show successes. You need to show a return on investment. You need to provide metrics. You need to provide accountability, because [legislators] are skeptical about investing in science and technology. Unless you can show them that this is more important than fixing the leaking roof in their elementary schools—or just as important—you're not going to get any support."

Bowles made an appeal to convocation participants who represent universities and laboratories to begin training individuals who can serve in advisory roles. "The set of skills that you need in influencing public policy is very different from the set of skills that you need to be a scientist," he said, "and we don't do a good job . . . of preparing people in how to interact appropriately with politicians or [interest] groups." Instead of preparing scientists and engineers solely for research positions, Bowles advocated that students be prepared for public service, rather than having them learn on the job. "A few people will go off and do that by themselves. But if we want to have a real impact, we need to set up some effective way of helping them, of supporting them, and [offering them] incentives."

Jay Cole, education policy advisor to Joe Manchin III, governor of West Virginia, suggested that the National Academies work with the National Governors Association to create a network of state science advisors. The members of the network could learn from others about what works and what does not. States that do not have a science and technology advisor could learn from interactions through the network what would be necessary to create and support such a position.

The set of skills that you need in influencing public policy is very different from the set of skills that you need to be a scientist, and we don't do a good job . . . of preparing people in how to interact appropriately with politicians or [interest] groups. Instead of preparing scientists and engineers solely for research positions, students [also should] be prepared for public service, rather than having them learn on the job. A few people will go off and do that by themselves. But if we want to have a real impact, we need to set up some effective way of helping them, of supporting them, and [offering them] incentives.

WORKING WITH STATE LEGISLATORS AND THEIR STAFFS

Matt Sundeen of the National Conference of State Legislatures,[2] which is a bipartisan nonprofit organization based in Denver with about 200 employees, spoke about his experience providing scientific and technological information to state legislators and their staffs to help inform their policy- and decision-making work.

There are currently 7,382 state legislators in the United States. Before the 2006 election, the split between Democrats and Republicans among legislators was about even; now Democrats exceed Republicans by about 650 (fewer than 100 state legislators have other party affiliations). The split between legislative control of the states is currently about even, with Democrats having a slight advantage.

State legislatures are very diverse, both within and among states. Some are full-time legislatures, but most are part-time. In some states, the legislature may meet for as little as one month a year and some meet just every two years. Bills are handled differently in different states, which can make it difficult to track issues from state to state. Also, many legislators do not have offices in their capitol buildings. "That makes it very difficult to go in and work with that lawmaker," Sundeen said, "because you're essentially trying to accost them in the hallway as opposed to actually sitting down in their office and presenting your case."

Legislators themselves are more diverse now than they have been in the past. About 26 percent are women, 8 percent are African American, and 3 percent are Latino. Because of term limits, legislators are getting younger on average, with an average age of 53, whereas the average age was more than 60 a decade ago. And 15 years ago, more than a quarter of

---

[2]For more information about the National Conference of State Legislatures, see <http://ncsl.org>.

legislators were attorneys, whereas now the percentage is about 15 percent. "We have farmers, auto mechanics, educators," said Sundeen. "We have people coming in from much more diverse backgrounds."

Beyond the legislators are about 35,000 legislative staff. Staff members, too, have a very wide range of responsibilities and backgrounds. Among the staff members are partisan staff, caucus staff, nonpartisan staff who are shared among legislators or legislative committees, research counsels, bill drafters, fiscal staff, committee staff, personal staff, administrative staff, interns, constituent relations staff, and so on. "You'll have to work with a lot of these people, and it's not the same in every state." Furthermore, while legislators turn over with each election—especially in states with term limits—many staff members remain in their positions for longer periods.

Almost all legislators and their staffs need help in dealing with science and technology policy issues. They may want enough neutral and honest information to establish a position on an issue. They also may be looking for information to support a position they already have established.

Legislators obviously affect state funding for research, Sundeen pointed out. But they also may affect other sources of funding that have an influence on research. By the same token, issues of funding tend to predominate on the legislative agenda. If an issue is not connected to the budget, it is less likely to get attention. When science and technology do rise to the surface in a legislative proposal not related to funding, it is often because the issues are politically charged, as with intelligent design creationism, stem cell research, or abortion. And, in these cases, legislators are likely to bring personal values to their deliberations that go well beyond the purely technical issues involved.

State legislators face a huge workload. More than 100,000 bills were considered in the 50 state legislatures in 2006. As a result, legislators are constantly bombarded with information and requests. "Everybody wants to tell them about their bill," said Sundeen, so legislators are plagued by "information overload."

One of the great advantages of working with state legislators is that they often are more accessible than their Washington, DC, counterparts, according to Sundeen. Furthermore, a state lawmaker may have a much more direct influence on a state or local issue than a federal lawmaker. "A lot of the federal policy decided in DC really doesn't have a direct impact on the everyday lives of the people in the states," Sundeen said. "But I think a lot that's done at the state legislative level has a very direct impact on the people within the state."

Sundeen offered convocation participants a number of tips for working effectively with legislators and their staffs:

- *Legislators need information that is actionable.* "You have to give them something that's actually something that they can do, that's within the authority of the state legislature to do, and it has to be given to them in a timely manner." Legislators and their staffs do not need a 200-page thesis, said Sundeen; they need a two-page brief, with model legislation, if possible.
- *Researchers need to be willing to meet with legislators and their staffs and provide expert testimony if requested.* "Politics is a very hands-on business. You have to be able to shake hands with people. And they have to be able to understand who you are, what you're dealing with, and what topic areas you know about."
- *Advocates and policy advisors need to establish relationships with legislators and their staffs early, before an issue becomes politically charged.* If a legislator is already bombarded with information, it will be difficult to get a word in edgewise. Orientation sessions for new members are especially valuable, since they provide an opportunity to establish personal relationships with incoming legislators. "From day one, you should be sending them information about your state academy of science or about your academic institution and let them know what you have to offer," said Sundeen. "Establish those relationships as early as you can, because if you wait until they're actually working on a bill, I think you're probably too late."
- *The minority party should not be ignored.* "Today's minority is tomorrow's majority," said Sundeen. Forging alliances with just one party or with policy makers who do not have much power can tie the hands of an advisor.
- *Information should be easy to understand, so policy makers know how it relates to an issue.* Policy advisors also should make clear what the limits are on the information being providing. They should know the opposing arguments about an issue and share them with a legislator. And when providing information to staff, it is best to make the extra effort to reach the appropriate staff member. The summer intern in a legislator's office, for example, is probably not the right person.

Sundeen recommended that policy advisors get feedback from legislators and members of their staffs. "It's not a one-way street," said Sundeen. Legislators and their staff have much to offer the science community. Policy advisors should ask legislators for advice, "even though you might not think you need it."

Finally, Sundeen suggested working closely with the constituents of a legislator. "Legislators want to get reelected," he said. "The axiom [is that] five letters makes it an issue. So if you can have five constituents contact their legislator about an issue, that makes it more important for the legislator."

The National Conference of State Legislatures has launched a new policy initiative to create permanent links between state legislatures and the science community. According to Sundeen, "we want to centralize some of the resources that we have on this issue [and] involve people from all sides." The goals of the project are to increase the quantity and quality of information going to legislators and legislative staff through such means as research, databases, site visits, technical assistance, briefings, papers, and so on. The National Conference of State Legislatures is also seeking feedback from legislators about the kinds of information they need, and the organization is tracking legislation to determine what kinds of science- and technology-related issues come up repeatedly in state legislatures.

John Unger—a state senator from West Virginia, an advisor to the U.S. Department of Energy's National Energy Technology Laboratory and the host of a public affairs radio talk show in West Virginia—emphasized the political side of policy making. There is often "a big disconnect between ideas and policy," he said. The best ideas do not necessarily always prevail. Politicians have other considerations. In particular, they often need to gauge public opinion and political pressures before they make a decision. As Unger put it, they have "a finger in the air testing the wind."

Given this reality of state policy making, "what we need to do is change the wind," said Unger. The great social and political movements of history have come about when ideas mobilized people and politicians responded. "Ideas matter," said Unger.

Because of the political aspects of policy making, Unger agreed with Sundeen that policy advisors can have a great impact by working through the constituents of a policy maker. Legislators want to serve their constituents well, both to do their jobs well and to get reelected. In both cases, they will be reflecting their constituents' desires.

Unger also emphasized the importance of working with newly elected legislators. Such legislators are often in the process of forming their legislative goals and agendas. "If you can convince them that your specific project or idea or whatever could be the difference, you'll have a champion then for life," said Unger.

Unger added that it is important to know who has the ear of the governor or a key legislator. Such a person might be in business, in education, in government, or elsewhere, but "those are the individuals you need to go and make an appoint to talk with." Ask for their advice and help, explaining your position carefully and clearly.

A particularly valuable approach is to have scientists and engineers work on model legislation, which then can be offered to policy makers. By replicating the process that lawmakers go through to write a bill, you "start thinking like a policy maker, and therefore it will help you to communicate with policy makers," said Unger. If members of the scientific and engineering communities feel that they are disenfranchised from the political process, working on model legislation can engage them in the process and empower them to seek change.

Scientists and engineers need to defend the integrity and value of their professions, Unger insisted. In politics, positions will be attacked by those who oppose a particular action. Even though professional rewards do not necessarily follow such actions, "you owe it to your profession to stand up and defend it," said Unger.

A final consideration, according to Unger, is that many different kinds of people need to be part of the decision-making process. Scientists or engineers may think that they know the correct answer. But when a broader spectrum of the stakeholders in a decision are brought into the process and made a part of the decision, a wider range of information is usually gathered. The decision that ensues may not necessarily be based entirely on scientific or technological considerations, but it will then have the support of the stakeholders. "You have to build those stakeholders processes, and when I say stakeholder I mean people for you and people against you. . . . And sometimes the answer may not be exactly what you want to go after, but you may get an answer that can work, and that's an important policy."

Several other convocation participants cited the value of working directly with legislators and offered ideas for how to make such meetings happen. William Harris, president of Science Foundation Arizona,[3] recounted that, when he was working in Ireland, he and a group of science and technology policy advisors met over breakfast about once a month with small groups of legislators who were interested in science. The discussions, which revolved around topics like vaccination, were informal but dealt with important subjects. "Scientists tend to talk to each other," said Harris, "and we don't invite politicians" into the conversation.

Lee Allison, the state geologist of Arizona, described an analogous program in Kansas.[4] Following each legislative session, legislators were offered a three-day field seminar in which they traveled by bus across the state looking at natural resources and environmental issues. The rule was

---

[3]For more information about Science Foundation Arizona, see <http://www.sfaz.org>.

[4]Articles describing the Kansas Field Conferences are available at <http://googledex.kgs. ku.edu/search?q=field+conference&site=kgs_main&client=kgs_main&proxystylesheet=kgs_ main&output=xml_no_dtd>.

that there could be no lobbying, just the exchange of information. The program organizers developed such a good relationship with the legislature that the chair of the House Energy and Natural Resources Committee asked the group to do a tutorial for the new members of the committee and freshman legislators on energy and resource issues. "We were in a position after 12 years of having a tremendous amount of credibility and contacts throughout the legislature, and they called on us routinely when they had questions because they knew we were going to give them straight answers," said Allison. When the New Mexico Geological Survey, which is based in Socorro, emulated the program, it was so successful that the legislators made it a formal committee meeting, so now all the committee members can attend the three-day field seminar. "It's a tremendous program," Allison said.

Sigma Xi has organized what it calls its Science Café programs,[5] where scientists and engineers make themselves available to talk with the public in a conversation, without slides or chalkboards. A straightforward extension of this program would be to organize Science Cafés for state legislators. "We just aren't targeting that particular audience at this point," said Kelly Sullivan. "So we could put the word out to our chapters to say this is another way we can serve the public understanding of science, which is one of our key missions."

Nancy Huddleston of the National Academies suggested that a survey of the executive and legislative branches of state governments be conducted to ascertain from where and how they get their information about science and technology. Based on the results of the survey, organizations could structure events and activities to provide legislators with information in the most effective ways.

---

[5]For more information about Science Cafés, see <http://www.sciencecafes.org/>.

State Legislatures: A Quiz

Scientists and engineers often claim that state legislators know relatively little about science and technology, so Matt Sundeen of the National Conference of State Legislators offered a quiz at the convocation to see how much the participants knew about state legislatures.

1. Which state chamber has the least number of members?

2. Which state legislative chamber has the most members?

3. Which legislature has the highest percentage of female legislators?

4. Which state has the highest capital in the United States?

5. Which state has the easternmost capital?

6. Which state in the continental United States has the southernmost capital?

7. Which four state capitals are named after U.S. presidents?

Answers: 1. Alaska. 2. New Hampshire. 3. Vermont. 4. New Mexico. 5. Maine. 6. Texas. 7. Lincoln, Nebraska; Madison, Wisconsin; Jefferson City, Missouri; Jackson, Mississippi.

Issue Focus: State Energy Policy

A set of breakout sessions at the convocation examined state science and technology policy advice specifically in the context of energy. Excerpts from one of the breakout sessions, while not part of the convocation's plenary sessions, demonstrate some of the ways in which science and technology policy advice come into play on a specific issue.

To provide sustainable energy without irrevocably damaging the environment, a wide range of energy options must be considered. Scientific and technological advice will be essential in determining the life-cycle costs and benefits of each source. If necessary information is not available, information gaps need to be identified and filled.

Some participants stated that nuclear power must be one of the energy options considered, and the same systematic and rational processes must be applied to it as to other potential energy sources. Potential problems, such as nuclear waste storage, must be identified, along with possible ways to resolve problems. Information also should be developed about plausible scenarios—if a particular action is not taken, what are the consequences?

By taking a comprehensive approach to an analysis of potential energy policies, comparisons can be made across options. Metrics that can enable these comparisons should be developed for each energy source, with comparable information about inputs and outcomes for each form of energy. Drawing a distinction between liquid transportation fuels and energy for power generation may be necessary, although trade-offs between the two exist.

Science and technology policy advice should try to anticipate how policy makers will respond to advice and what they will say to their constituents. Policy makers are more interested in short-term, tactical information than they are in long-term, strategic information, and they are more likely to act on the former.

The political context differs among states, and these differences need to be taken into account. However, many issues are the same or comparable across state lines, enabling collaborative efforts and standardization. For issues that cut across state boundaries, the National Academies and other national organizations can act as arbiters, validators of findings and results, and sources of information. National organizations also can convene regional meetings to examine issues shared among states.

5

Communicating Science and Technology Policy Advice Effectively

Aset of presentations that focused on ways for scientists and engineers to become more effective communicators of science and technology policy advice engendered a great deal of discussion at the convocation. Participants examined whether and how to "frame" scientific and technological information, the need to take a stand on critical issues, and how best to work with the media.

> *There is often a big disconnect between ideas and policy. The best ideas do not necessarily always prevail. Politicians have other considerations. In particular, they often need to gauge public opinion and political pressures before they make a decision. As Unger put it, they have a finger in the air testing the wind.*

FRAMING THE ISSUES

In a recent issue of *Science*, Matthew Nisbet, an assistant professor of communication at American University in Washington, DC, and writer Chris Mooney published an article that called for a reexamination of the way scientists and engineers communicate information to the public (Nisbet and Mooney, 2007). In his presentation, Nisbet elaborated on their views and responded to some of the reactions their article has provoked.

Their article questioned what Nisbet called the "popular science model"—the idea that if the public only knew more about science, it would view issues as scientists do.

This model calls for improving science education, which of course is vitally important to the nation for a number of reasons, Nisbet said. It also calls for continued education of the adult population through the popular science media. The assumption is that if science literacy is boosted through the media, "there will be fewer controversies between science and society, and policy makers will be more likely to support science," Nisbet said. The model for such an effort is Carl Sagan. "We hear over and over again that . . . if we only had more scientists like Carl Sagan, those problems would go away."

There are two major problems with this model, said Nisbet. The first is that decades of social science research have shown that most people do not arrive at decisions in the way posited by the popular science model. Instead of being well motivated to learn more about science-related issues, most people, including many policy makers, use various cognitive screening mechanisms to make decisions. They rely on shortcuts, heuristics, ideology, or emotions to make up their minds, often without knowing much about the issue they are considering. National political campaigns understand this very well and have adopted principles from this research into their campaign strategies. The 2004 Bush campaign did not run on the complexities of the issues so much as on the character and likeability of the candidate, Nisbet contended. "The internal strategy that the Bush campaign used or modeled went something like this: If he doesn't fit your life, share your values, or isn't someone you want to have a beer with, then he shouldn't be your President."

The second problem with the popular science model is that it doesn't fit well with the structure of the modern media system, Nisbet observed. The paradox today is not that there are too few sources of information—there are too many. "In 1985 if you sat down to watch television at six o'clock, you really only had four choices available to you, and all four of those choices involved public affairs news with some steady amount of science news. But if you sat down to watch TV at six o'clock in 2007, there are almost 300 different cable channels from which to select. If you lack a strong comfort for public affairs and science content, you can very easily pay attention only to 'infotainment,' entertainment, or, in some cases, the ideologically or religiously preferred views of different channels."

Given the failings of the popular science model, how can proponents of science reach the public while remaining true to the science? In their article, Nisbet and Mooney suggested using research on "framing theory" as a way to complement investments in formal education and good science media. In essence, framing means thinking about how best to present an issue to a particular audience. With a complex issue, a communicator focuses on certain dimensions of that issue over other dimensions. The focus might be why the issue is a problem, who or what might be responsible, or what should be done about it. Furthermore, this focus is reinforced using slogans, historical references, cartoons, or images. "When you structure information in a press release or a report, there are multiple options available to you that are equally consistent with the science in terms of the types of examples that you can bring to bear," said Nisbet. "And it makes sense to do research in terms of focus groups with an intended audience about which of those multiple examples make the issue most personally meaningful."

Journalists rely on framing all the time to organize their stories and inform their audiences, said Nisbet. In turn, readers, viewers, and listeners learn from media interpretations that closely resonate with their social backgrounds.

Policy makers at the federal, state, and local levels also use frames as a way to define policy issues in ways that favor their preferred positions. In addition, they may rely on frames to make up their minds about a piece of legislation, and sometimes their decisions are attacked by others using different frames.

Framing can be directed toward different goals and outcomes, Nisbet pointed out. It may seek to increase the size of the audience interested in science. It may be designed to create polarization in a particular debate, thus shaping preferences for policies informed by science. Framing also may be used to enhance trust in science or shape personal or political behavior. For example, in his book *The Creation*, E.O. Wilson (2006) intuitively uses framing very effectively, according to Nisbet. The book is about environmental conservation, but Wilson casts the book as a moral message delivered on a personal level to a Southern Baptist minister. "In the process he has introduced popular science about conservation to an audience of religious Americans who might not otherwise pay attention to that problem."

Research has shown that particular frames recur in policy debates involving science and technology. For example, science and technology are often defined in terms of positive social qualities that make our lives better and boost the economy, particularly when the underlying issue is national, state, or local competitiveness. When science is opposed, it tends to be depicted as an out-of-control monster that will create either physical or moral disasters. Sometimes science is depicted in terms of uncertainty, a tactic often used by those who advocate intelligent design creationism or who are skeptical about global warming. And other times science is associated with public accountability.

All of these instances of framing have occurred in the debate over research using stem cells, Nisbet pointed out, particularly as it played out in California before the Proposition 71 initiative on stem cell research. The organizers of the proposition campaign knew that they were not going to break through to the wider public by narrowly focusing on the technical parts of the research or by bringing the public up to speed on the science. They also understood that attacking the public for opposing the research because of religious beliefs would not be effective. Instead, they recast the issues in ways that emphasized shared common values, social progress, the potential for new medical therapies, and economic development for the state. They used scientists as spokespeople, but they also teamed up with nonresearchers, like actor Brad Pitt, and they used the media to reach nontraditional audiences for science.

"Here's a great example of how they did this," said Nisbet. "Brad Pitt appeared on NBC's Today Show in October 2004. When asked by Katie Couric why he supported Proposition 71, he first focused on the social part of his message as one of extraordinary opportunity if you have a disease. Second, he focused on the idea of economic development—that California is losing scientists to places like Singapore. And when Couric then asked him to talk about his new movie, he didn't stray off topic but came back and reemphasized the economic progress message focusing on the fact that this is not a cost to California, but rather an investment in the future."

The proponents of Proposition 71 were also successful because they used their money well. They raised more than $20 million and spent that amount on meaningful ads in California, while the opposition spent only about $200,000. Although polls in August indicated about equal support and opposition to the proposition, by November it passed with 59 percent of the vote.

However, the proponents of the proposition sometimes exceeded the bounds of currently available evidence, Nisbet pointed out. When John Edwards was campaigning in 2004 as the vice presidential nominee, he said that stem cell research would enable Christopher Reeve to get up out of his wheelchair and walk. That was "going too far in terms of what the timeline for actual therapies might be," Nisbet said.

On the other side of the debate, the opponents of the proposition knew that attacking the moral status of stem cell research would resonate only with their base, not with the broader public. To capture the middle ground, they cast the debate in terms of public accountability. The same thing happened with an ultimately successful campaign to amend the state constitution in Missouri to protect stem cell research. Opponents asked whether stem cell research serves the private interest or the public interest, used catch phrases like "big biotech," and asked who was going to watch the scientists.

Successful framing requires research on how nontraditional audiences perceive science and what aspects of complex science debates are personally meaningful to them. On the basis of those results, further research can explore which phrases, examples, and metaphors succeed best in conveying that meaning. Data on public opinion that is more localized would be very useful in this effort, Nisbet noted. Although the National Science Foundation regularly publishes analyses of public attitudes about science in its *Science Indicators* reports, there are no state-level polling data about science. "A useful project would be to put together resources and apply for grant money to try to target key states, and look across key states in terms of gathering comparative methods on public opinions, state poll reviews, and meaningful ways to inform a broader public debate and communication," Nisbet said.

Effective framing also requires that there be "a lot of coordination and discipline in how you apply these messages," said Nisbet. National communication campaigns need to be coordinated, whether the topic is stem cell research or climate change. The message at the national level needs to be coordinated with the message at state and local levels. Proponents of a position then need to be very good at getting into local newspapers and appearing on televisions shows. Polls show that the number one source of public affairs programming for about 65 percent of Americans is the local news, so scientists, spokespeople, and other organization leaders should seek especially to cultivate contacts with local media outlets.

Recruiting and training of opinion leaders is another effective approach in framing scientific and technological issues, Nisbet said. These opinion leaders can convince members of the public to pay closer attention to science, and they are very good at passing information to others and convincing others to adopt a certain position.

In such cities as Seattle, New York, and San Francisco, universities are collaborating with science media and graduate students at universities to create regional hubs for science communication. In particular, universities "are increasingly seeing evening programs as a very important way to generate adult programming and regional collaboration in science."

Universities and other institutions also are using new media like blogs and networking sites to make learning about science a social activity. According to Nisbet, every university research communication office should have a blog that focuses on the local dimensions of science in the community. There is a demand for local news about science, but people need a place to go for that news. Also, "one of the ways that science organizations can effectively use blogs is as a fact check function," Nisbet observed. "So when reports are released by institutions or there's breaking science news and there's distortion in the coverage, that's a way to [track] reports, correct distortions, and have something that's up and that's quick. It takes institutional investment and a staff person who's good at running the blog. But I think blogs can be very effective as a direct communication tool."

It also is important to have strong relationships with churches, temples, and mosques. "As many of you know across the country, churches are very important places for communication not only about personal and social issues but also policy issues," Nisbet said. "Scientists and scientific leaders should be visible as spokespeople at churches, and religious leaders should be invited to speak at universities and research institutions."

Documentary films on issues involving science and technology can be excellent communication tools, as evidenced by the success of Al Gore's movie *An Inconvenient Truth*. "Teaming with filmmakers or film producers to bring films and scenes to the local community—and staging forums around these films—is a very important way to not only inform people about science [but] also to make the science social and to build community interaction," Nisbet said.

Not everyone at the convocation agreed that the framing of issues in science and technology is desirable. "I think that [framing] is a detriment, quite frankly," said Lynn Elfner. To influence policy, it may be necessary to find a "hook" in the journalistic sense to communicate a position. "But I know from experience that the more you're an advocate for something, the less you are respected for the information you're presenting," Elfner said. "If you get billed as having a narrow position, then your credibility is going to go down the tubes."

Pister noted that scientists and engineers can adopt a range of positions in the framing of issues. Quoting from a recent book by Roger Pielke (2007), he cited four idealized models for the role of a scientist. First is the disinterested pure scientist who does not get involved in policy discussions. Second is the science arbiter who provides expertise on narrowly defined and testable questions. Third is the honest broker who provides a suite of scientifically informed policy options "in much the same way that a travel guide provides information on restaurants or hotels in unfamiliar territory," Pister said. And fourth is the overt advocate for a position. "Those four categories really cover the . . . space of information that we're trying to transmit to people," said Pister.

WHEN SCIENTISTS TAKE A STAND

Marla Cone, a reporter at the *Los Angeles Times*, began her presentation at the convocation with a story.

> I want to start by telling all of you a tale of two countries. [In] one country in the early 1990s, scientists were testing breast milk for contaminants—it

was something they regularly do there—and to their alarm, they found a big surge of concentrations of certain compounds in the breast milk. These compounds are called PBDEs [polybrominated biphenyl ether]. They are flame retardants. They are used in furniture and carpets and furniture cushions, electronics, plastics, those types of things, and these scientists were very concerned. These chemicals were structurally similar to PCBs [polychlorinated biphenyl] and most of the world had already gone through a nightmare of trying to clean up PCBs.

They were very troubled about this. They hadn't yet published their work, but they met with government leaders and they talked with a sense of urgency and concern about what they found. And soon, in the mid-1990s, industry there voluntarily stopped using these compounds. After that, the government there banned them. . . . By 1998, a year before these scientists [published] their work, the concentrations in breast milk in those countries began to decline. Now that is a success story. It was a big success story long before the scientists even published their data.

Then I want to tell you about another country, one that doesn't regularly monitor breast milk. Similar problems were found with PBDEs, but concentrations were far worse, much higher than in that other country. They were 10 to 100 times higher back in the 1990s, yet no action was taken, and the levels kept growing throughout the 1990s until about 2004. These levels were the highest anywhere. No other country had levels as high as this particular country.

As you probably know by now, that first country is in Europe—it's Sweden—and they took immediate action based on the input of their scientists. The second country, of course, is the United States. No immediate action was taken. There was very little input from scientists and a long delay in any kind of intervention.

Finally, California took action and banned these compounds in 2004, which was almost a decade after the European phase-out. Other states have followed. The EPA finally agreed and set a voluntary agreement with the chemical manufacturers to ban those particular compounds. And now levels here are finally starting to decline as they did in Europe a decade earlier.

The lesson for scientists, said Cone, is that they can have a big effect on policy when they are willing to speak out about what they have found. "Scientists in Europe often don't wait," said Cone. "They don't pull their punches. They don't need decades of human or animal testing and often base what they're telling the public on the precautionary principle, which is better safe than sorry." In the United States, in contrast, policy makers and scientists usually assume that a particular environmental threat is innocent until proven guilty.

Scientists in the United States need to speak out when they think it is necessary to do so, Cone contended. If they feel a need for urgency, they need to communicate that urgency. That has finally started to happen in the United States with PBDEs, Cone said. "Scientists have finally gotten more vocal about it, more certain, talking about the certainties rather than the uncertainties. I think that's very important because scientists often talk about the limitations of their research, which is important to get across. But you also have to talk about what you're certain about."

A particularly effective tool for communicating scientific assurance is a consensus statement, Cone contended. Such reports have led to progress on the regulation of endocrine disrupters (chemicals that influence the levels or internal regulation of one or more hormones in animals or humans) and other chemicals in the environment. A consensus approach says "here's what we know, here's what we think we know, here's what we don't know. . . . That is the perfect format for a journalist like me who's trying to untangle it all."

Scientists also need to be wary of mixed messages, according to Cone. For example, people have become very confused about the effects of mercury in fish. The media have a tendency to polarize issues and present diametrically opposed positions, which can further confuse readers, viewers, or listeners. "An important message for scientists, as well as government leaders . . . is that there may be polarized sides on this issue, but there's also a happy medium."

Technical experts can learn from organizations that help them communicate their messages. That's more effective than, for example, asking reporters for a list of questions before an interview, which gets in the way of developing a personal relationship between a reporter and a source, Cone said. What's needed is for scientists and engineers "to have some basic guidelines and training, so they're more comfortable talking with reporters and they're not afraid of saying the wrong thing."

VIEWS FROM THE TRENCHES

Bill Hammack, a professor of chemical and biomolecular engineering at the University of Illinois, Urbana-Champaign, who has worked both at the U.S. Department of State and as a regular commentator for public radio,[1] offered several rules for working with the media. One is to always keep the social, political, economic, and cultural context in mind, not just the technical details. He quoted G.K. Chesterton: "The only two things that can satisfy the soul are a person and a story; and even a story must be about a person." When scientists and engineers are interacting with the

---

[1] For additional information about this public radio show ("Engineering and Life"), see <http://engineerguy.com>.

media, they have to remember the power of stories. "This is meant to be a little polemical," he said. "Stop reading about science and engineering. You know enough. There are other skills you need."

Despite the fragmentation of the media, radio and television still have many viewers and listeners, Hammack pointed out. The public radio show "Morning Edition" reaches 12 million people, which is 8 to 10 times the circulation of the *New York Times.*

Hammack observed that policy and decision makers also get a considerable amount of information from think tanks, partly because these types of organizations specialize in tailoring their advice for policy prescriptions. Also, think tanks employ many ex- and future government officials. They "rotate in and out and are comfortable there."

Still, the print media have a disproportionate influence for elected officials because they can access it very quickly. Politicians and their staffs read the newspaper every day, said John McDonald, another member of the convocation's panel on communicating science as well as president and owner of the strategic communications company Stone's Throw. Newspapers are "the first frame of the debate," said McDonald. "They shape radio. They shape television broadcasts. They even drive the blogosphere." Newspaper coverage "gives you instant credibility," McDonald continued. It "opens the door to further conversation."

As a principal at a communications company, McDonald specializes in the placement of ideas. "I work with reporters a lot. I talk to them. I try to get them interested in important stuff, and I try to get them to write about it in meaningful ways that are interesting. [Then] I try to get policy makers to read it and make sure they look at it. And in doing that, I'm trying to open the doors for further conversations between people like you and the policy-making community."

The most important thing for scientists and engineers to do is to engage in the process, according to McDonald. "As scientists, you need to join the battle if people are going to pay attention to the work that you do. . . . You're going to have to engage." This sounds like obvious advice, he admitted, but sometimes it is hard advice for the scientific and academic communities to grasp. "You spend most of your time talking to each other."

In talking with members of the public, scientists and engineers have to do so in ways "that are meaningful to their lives—not to your life, to their lives." Such conversations are important, because powerful organizations are spending millions of dollars to shape the debate. "If you're not doing that work, if you're not part of the conversation, then your message isn't going to get out there," McDonald said. "And remember, the first rule of politics is to define yourself because if you don't do it, the other guy will."

In talking with members of the public, scientists and engineers have to do so in ways that are meaningful to their lives—not to your life.

McDonald is not overly concerned with frames. "They have their place," McDonald said. "But I'm not sure they're for people like you, to be honest." Framing is a sophisticated technique that is best done as part of communications campaigns. Content is king, he said, and content is where science and technology excel. "As scientists and engineers, you need to be able to tell people what you're doing, why it's important, and what needs to be done about it. . . . The greatest asset you bring to the table is knowledge and expertise." Sharing this expertise in clear, concise, and compassionate terms requires work, money, and commitment. Scientists and engineers need to think about what to communicate, who they need to communicate with, and what they need to say. "You're the experts. That's your job. That's what you need to do."

Finally, scientists and engineers have to be available to talk with reporters, and not just when they have something to communicate. In particular, reporters are much less likely to be accommodating if scientists and engineers duck questions that are uncomfortable. Scientists and engineers also need to be ready to be criticized. "Sometimes people get paid a lot of money to say very harsh things about you and your work. So if you're going to venture out there, be sure your i's are dotted, your t's are crossed, and have a thick skin," McDonald said.

6

Next Steps to Enhance Science and Technology Policy Advice at the State Level

To forge a more effective science and technology policy advising system at the state level, many presenters and participants at the convocation thought that changes must occur both inside and outside government.

According to Doug Henton, states must place themselves in a position to take advantage of science and technology policy advice more effectively and efficiently. First, state governments need to work with academic institutions and businesses to identify the state's strengths and weaknesses. "What are your strengths? What do you want to be good at? What do you want to build on? What are your assets?"

The state then must invest in institutions and programs that enable it to take advantage of its strengths and minimize its weaknesses. The key is not necessarily how much a state spends, Henton said, but how funding is used. For example, state support can be used to foster collaboration and long-term commitments. "You don't want to do one thing and the next thing and the next thing," Henton said. The centers of scientific and technological development in states that have been successful, such as Research Triangle Park in North Carolina,[1] are products of sustained and long-term investments.

Outside state governments, the institutions that are in a position to offer science and technology policy advice at the state level must

---

[1]For more information about North Carolina's Research Triangle Park, see <http://www.rtp.org/main>.

work together and learn from each other. Colleges and universities, other nonprofit research institutions, federal laboratories, state academies of science, and state science and technology councils can all act to enhance the science and technology base in a state and connect that base to the state's goals. Furthermore, all of these institutions are working effectively in some states and not others. A mechanism for sharing best practices and innovative approaches could strengthen policy advice in all states.

States need to establish systems to measure the results of initiatives involving science and technology. Once money is spent, the legislature and governor are going to ask what was accomplished and why the state should continue to fund these activities. Again, some states already have made considerable progress. For example, the Massachusetts Innovation Index measures every step of the innovation process, including research and development, commercialization, patents, royalties, and outputs in terms of new jobs. Measures should not include just inputs but also outputs in terms of facilities, patents, personnel, education, and so on. Other possible measures are industry interactions, collaborations, invention disclosures, licensing, venture capital attracted, new companies formed, industry concentrations increased, companies retained, employment increased, the number of high-value-added jobs created, graduate students hired in the state, existing industries transformed, and new industries developed. "There needs to be some type of an accounting system in place," said Henton. "Promises can't be made for future results. Results need to be measured from the outset of an effort."

HISTORY IN THE MAKING

"The United States is entering a new era of scientific and technological development, one where the states assume a much greater role than has been the case in the past," said Jay Cole. "We are fairly early in the history of the state science and technology policy movement, and recognizing this also allows us in a sense to recognize that we're making this history. We're in uncharted territory, and we need to learn from everything we're doing so that we continue to make progress in the future."

Participants were particularly enthusiastic to recreate the dynamism and synergy of the convocation. "We've been hoping to have a meeting of this sort for many years," said Susan Hackwood. Although California has had an active state-level science and technology policy advising system, it has known little about what other states are doing, and "for us that's been a big handicap, so I'm delighted for this meeting." According to Gerry O'Keefe, "This kind of meeting is unique. I've learned a great deal, and I think my colleagues have learned a great deal. . . . Kudos to the National

Academies for doing this. . . . It's a great service to the country and a great service to the states getting this group of people together.

Future meetings that bring together people from across the country could be sponsored by the National Academies, perhaps with a focus on different topics that are important to all the states. In addition, regional meetings of nearby states could be extremely valuable, said Hackwood. "If you put a regional meeting together that brought together academics, lots of industry people, and most importantly policy people, the people who are in the trenches working with legislatures, working with the governor's office, and making policy, if you bring these people together, the chemistries that will happen and the ideas that will come out, I guarantee you, will be quite remarkable."

Regional meetings would enable states to learn from the policy work done in nearby states. "If we [in California] have done a study on regional climate change, how can it be used in Arizona?" Hackwood said. "If Arizona's done a study on nanotech, how can it be used in California? And how can that connect into National Academies studies, because that's a root source of a lot of this information. There's no competition between our states. We have everything to gain by learning from each other."

The states are often called "laboratories for democracy," said Edward Derrick, the director of the Research Competitiveness Program for the American Association for the Advancement of Science.[2] The same is true of science and technology policy advice. "The opportunity here as scientists is to learn from the experiments that are going on in the states in science policy and science policy advising," Derrick said. National and regional meetings could serve as forums for the horizontal diffusion of successful experiments. At the same time, there are commonalities among states, and "I believe that's been proved by this discussion."

Karl Pister quoted the comic strip Pogo saying, "we are surrounded by walls of insurmountable opportunity." The convocation helped make those walls surmountable. "We need good advice from people who understand how to put scaling ladders on those walls," Pister said.

---

[2]For more information about AAAS's Research Competitiveness Program, see <http://www.aaas.org/spp/rcp>.

References

Bush, V. (1945). *Science—The Endless Frontier: A Report to the President*. Washington, DC: U.S. Government Printing Office. Available: http://www.nsf.gov/od/lpa/nsf50/vbush1945.htm [accessed Feb. 2008].

National Academy of Sciences, National Academy of Engineering, and Institute of Medicine. (2007). *Rising Above the Gathering Storm: Energizing and Employing America for a Brighter Economic Future*. Committee on Prospering in the Global Economy of the 21st Century: An Agenda for American Science and Technology. Committee on Science, Engineering, and Public Policy. Washington, DC: The National Academies Press. Available: http://www.nap.edu/catalog.php?record_id=11463 [accessed Feb. 2008].

National Research Council. (2004). *Managing the Columbia River: Instream Flows, Water Withdrawals, and Salmon Survival*. Committee on Water Resources Management, Instream Flows, and Salmon Survival in the Columbia River Basin. Water Science and Technology Board. Board on Environmental Studies and Toxicology. Division on Earth and Life Studies. Washington, DC: The National Academies Press. Available: http://www.nap.edu/catalog.php?record_id=10962 [accessed Feb. 2008].

National Research Council. (2007). *Enhancing Professional Development for Teachers: Potential Uses of Information Technology. Report of a Workshop*. National Academies Teacher Advisory Council. Center for Education, Division of Behavioral and Social Sciences and Education. Washington, DC: The National Academies Press. Available: http://www.nap.edu/catalog.php?record_id=11995 [accessed Feb. 2008].

Nisbet, M.C., and Mooney, C. (2007). Science and society: Framing science. *Science, 316*(5821), 56. Available: http://www.sciencemag.org/cgi/content/full/316/582156?maxtoshow=&HITS=10&hits=10& RESULTFORMAT=&andorexacttitleabs=and&andorexactfulltext=and&searchid=1&FIRSTINDEX=0&volume=316&firstpage=56&resourcetype=HWCIT [accessed Feb. 2008].

Pew Center on the States. (2007). *Investing in Innovation*. Washington, DC: National Governors Association. Available: http://www.nga.org/Files/pdf/0707INNOVATIONINVEST.PDF [accessed Feb. 2008].

Pielke, R.A., Jr. (2007). *The Honest Broker: Making Sense of Science in Policy and Politics*. New York: Cambridge University Press.

Wilson, E.O. (2006). *The Creation: An Appeal to Save Life on Earth*. New York: W.W. Norton.

Appendix A

Convocation Agenda

State Science and Technology Policy Advice:
Issues, Assets, and Opportunities

Convocation #1: Energy, Environment, and Economic Competitiveness
Hosted by the
National Academy of Sciences,
the National Academy of Engineering,
the Institute of Medicine,
the National Association of Academies of Science,
and the California Council on Science and Technology
Arnold and Mabel Beckman Center, Irvine, CA

Day One (Monday, October 15, 2007)

8:30 to 8:45 a.m.
Welcoming Remarks
- *Karl Pister, Dean and Roy W. Carlson Professor of Engineering Emeritus, University of California, Berkeley, and member of the National Academy of Engineering*
- *Kenneth Fulton, Executive Director, National Academy of Sciences*

8:45 to 9:15 a.m.
Keynote Address
Richard Atkinson, President Emeritus, University of California, and member of the National Academy of Sciences and Institute of Medicine
→The Increasing Importance of State Roles in Science & Technology (S&T) (focus on energy and environment)
→The Importance of S&T Information and Advice for Policy Making

9:15 to 10:00 a.m.
An Overview of the Current State S&T Policy Landscape
Doug Henton, President, Collaborative Economics
→Summary of the Report on State Investment in R&D from the Pew Center on the States

10:00 to 10:15 a.m.
Break

10:15 to 11:00 a.m.
Case Study—The Importance of Scientific Evidence for Developing
Policies to Manage the Columbia River Basin in Washington
*Gerry O'Keefe, Columbia River Policy Coordinator, Washington State
Department of Ecology*

11:00 a.m. to 12:30 p.m.
Panel Discussion—Sources of S&T Information and Evidence for State-
Level Policy Making
Panelists:
- *Susan Hackwood, Executive Director, California Council on Science and
  Technology*
- *Lynn Elfner, Executive Director, Ohio Academy of Science*
- *Len Peters, Vice President, Battelle*
- *Warren Muir, Executive Director, Division on Earth and Life Studies,
  National Research Council*

12:30 to 1:30 p.m.
Lunch-Dining Room

1:30 to 1:45 p.m.
Afternoon Orientation
Karl Pister

1:45 to 3:15 p.m.
Panel Discussion—Differing Roles and Needs for S&T Information and
Advice
Panelists:
- *Thomas Bowles, Science Advisor to Governor Bill Richardson, New
  Mexico*
- *John Unger, State Senator, West Virginia*
- *Matt Sundeen, National Conference of State Legislatures*
- *Larry McKinney, Director of Coastal Fisheries, Texas Parks and Wildlife
  Department*

3:15 to 3:30 p.m.
Break and Proceed to Breakout Sessions

3:30 to 5:00 p.m.
Breakout Session #1: Meeting the Needs of Policy Makers for S&T
Information and Advice
Topics:
→Energy
→Environment
- *Jay Cole, Education Policy Advisor to the Governor of West Virginia (Facilitator)*
- *William Harris, President and CEO, Science Foundation, Arizona (Facilitator)*

Participants will be assigned to one or the other of these sessions so that
a balance of expertise is achieved in each. Economic implications will be
a thread of discussion in each session.

5:00 to 5:10 p.m.
Return from Breakouts to Plenary Session

5:10 to 5:30 p.m.
Closing Remarks, Discussion, and Overview of Day Two

Day Two (Tuesday, October 16, 2007)

8:30 to 8:45 a.m.
Orientation and Questions from Previous Day
Karl Pister

8:45 to 10:15 a.m.
Presentation and Discussion: Effectively Communicating S&T
Information and Evidence to State Policy Makers
- *Matt Nisbet, American University (via videoconference)*
- *Marla Cone, Los Angeles Times*
- *William Hammack, Professor of Engineering, University of Illinois*
- *John McDonald, President, Stone's Throw Strategic Communications*

10:15 to 10:30 a.m.
Break and Proceed to Breakout Sessions

10:30 a.m. to 12:00 p.m.
Breakout Session #2: State and Regional Planning
This session will allow participants to integrate the information and
discussions from this convocation to undertake initial planning about
how various science organizations from each region can begin to work
more closely together. Participants will be assigned to sessions based on
their geographic region.

12:00 to 12:10 p.m.
Return from Breakout Sessions to Final Plenary

12:10 to 12:45 p.m.
Concluding Remarks and Next Steps for Future Convocations, Communications, and Networking
* *Karl Pister*
* *Edward Derrick, Director, Competitiveness Programs, American Association for the Advancement of Science*
* *Members of the Convocation Organizing Committee*

12:45 p.m.
Adjourn

Appendix B

Convocation Participants

PRESENTERS AND FACILITATORS

Richard C. Atkinson
President Emeritus
University of California
San Diego, CA

Holly Harris Bane
Associate Vice President for
    Strategic Initiatives and
    Engagement
University of Akron
Akron, OH

Thomas Bowles
Science Advisor to New Mexico
    Governor Bill Richardson
New Mexico Governor's Office
Santa Fe, NM

Jay Cole
Education Advisor to West
    Virginia Governor Joe
    Manchin III
Charleston, WV

Marla Cone
Environmental Writer
Los Angeles Times
Los Angeles, CA

Edward Derrick
Director, AAAS Research
    Competitiveness Program
American Association for the
    Advancement of Science
Washington, DC

Kenneth Fulton
Executive Director
National Academy of Sciences
Washington, DC

Susan Hackwood
Executive Director
California Council on Science &
    Technology
Riverside, CA

William Hammack
University of Illinois
Department of Chemical and
    Biomolecular Engineering
Urbana, IL

William C. Harris
President and CEO
Science Foundation Arizona
Phoenix, AZ

Doug Henton
President & CEO
Collaborative Economics
Mountain View, CA

John McDonald
President
Stone's Throw Strategic
    Communications
Manhattan Beach, CA

Larry McKinney
Director of Coastal Fisheries
Texas Parks and Wildlife
    Department
Austin, TX

Warren Muir
Executive Director
Division on Earth and Life Studies
National Research Council
Washington, DC

Matthew C. Nisbet
    Assistant Professor
School of Communication
American University
Washington, DC

Gerry O'Keefe
Columbia River Policy
    Coordinator
Washington State Department of
    Ecology
Olympia, WA

Len Peters
Vice President
Battelle Memorial Institute
Columbus, OH

Karl Pister
Chairman of the Board
California Council on Science and
    Technology
Berkeley, CA

Matt Sundeen
Program Principal
National Conference of State
    Legislatures
Denver, CO

Honorable John Unger
State Senator
West Virginia State Senate
Martinsburg, WV

PLANNING COMMITTEE

Jay Cole
Education Policy Advisor
Office of the Governor
Charleston, WV

Lynn Elfner
Chief Executive Officer
The Ohio Academy of Science
Columbus, OH

Donna Gerardi Riordan
Director of Programs
California Council on Science and
    Technology
Capitola, CA

Nancy Huddleston
Senior Communications Officer
Division on Earth and Life Studies
National Research Council
Washington, DC

Jay Labov
Senior Advisor for Education and
    Communication
National Academy of Sciences
Washington, DC

Karl Pister
Chairman of the Board
California Council on Science and
    Technology
Berkeley, CA

PARTICIPANTS

Bruce Alberts
Department of Biochemistry and
    Biophysics
University of California
San Francisco, CA

Lee Allison
State Geologist and Director
Arizona Geological Survey
Tucson, AZ

Jameel Alsalam
Student
University of California
Berkeley, CA

John Burch
Investor
Ergosyst Associates, Inc.
Lawrence, KS

Richard Canino
Researcher
New Energy and Industrial
    Technology Development
    Organization
Washington, DC

Matthew Case
Graduate Student
Goldman School of Public Policy
University of California
Berkeley, CA

Elizabeth Chornesky
Analyst, Independent Consultant
Carmel, CA

Janet DeMint
Distinctive Voices Program
    Administrator
National Academy of Sciences
Irvine, CA

Jim Earthman
Associate Vice Chancellor for
    Research
University of California
Irvine, CA

Jenny Gautier
Program Coordinator
University of California
Office of the President
Oakland, CA

Phil Geis
Scientist
Ohio Academy of Science
Cincinnati, OH

M.R.C. Greenwood
Chancellor Emerita, University of
    California, Santa Cruz
University of California
Davis, CA

Edward Haddad
Executive Director
Florida Academy of Sciences
Orlando, FL

Holly Harris Bane
Associate Vice President for
    Strategic Initiatives and
    Engagement
University of Akron
Akron, OH

Mary Haskins
Executive Director
Missouri Academy of Science
Kansas City, MO

Paul Hill
Program Director
West Virginia EPSCoR
Charleston, WV

James Hoehn
Senior Associate
EPSCoR/IDeA Foundation
Santa Monica, CA

Paul Jennings
Professor of Civil Engineering and
    Applied Mechanics
California Institute of Technology
Pasadena, CA

Craig Johnson
Executive Director
Iowa Academy of Science
Cedar Falls, IA

Scott Jordan
Department of Computer Science
University of California
Irvine, CA

Lee Langston
Professor Emeritus of Mechanical
    Engineering
University of Connecticut
Storrs, CT

Annzell Loufas
Director, Sacramento Office
California Council on Science &
    Technology
Sacramento, CA

Charles Lytle
President, North Carolina
    Academy of Science and
    Professor, Zoology
North Carolina State University
Biology Outreach Programs
Raleigh, NC

Amber Mace
Executive Director
California Ocean Science Trust
Oakland, CA

Cathie Magowan
Director, Science, Engineering,
    and Technology Research
    Programs
University of California Office of
    the President
Oakland, CA

Lora Lee Martin
Director, Special Projects
University of California
Santa Cruz, CA

Tunyalee Martin
Multicampus Research Program
    Coordinator
University of California
Office of the President
Oakland, CA

Robert (Bob) McMahan
State Science and Technology
    Advisor
State of North Carolina
Raleigh, NC

Jennifer Mendez
Manager, Governmental Issues
Carpet and Rug Institute
Arlington, VA

Robin Newmark
External Relations, Global Security
Lawrence Livermore National
    Laboratory
Livermore, CA

Steve Olson
Writer
Bethesda, MD

Arthur Pontau
Senior Manager
Materials and Energy Sciences
Sandia National Laboratories
Livermore, CA

R. Sean Randolph
President and CEO
Bay Area Economic Forum
San Francisco, CA

George Scalise
President
Semiconductor Industry
    Association
San Jose, CA

Karen Scott
Government Relations
Sandia National Laboratories
Livermore, CA

Kjell Sehlstedt
Researcher
Swedish Association of Graduate
    Engineers
Swedish Office of Science &
    Technology
Los Angeles, CA

Kelly Sullivan
Director, Institutional Partnerships
Pacific Northwest National
    Laboratory
Richland, WA

Veronica Villalobos
Director, State Government
    Relations
University of Southern California
Sacramento, CA

Michele Wheatly
Dean
Wright State University
Dayton, OH

Kip Wiley
Deputy Director
Senate Office of Research
State of California
Sacramento, CA

Gareth Wynn-Williams
Professor of Astronomy
Institute for Astronomy
Hawaii Academy of Science
Honolulu, HI

Stephen Young
Instructor
Morningside High School
Inglewood, CA

Appendix C

Biographical Sketches of Presenters and Facilitators

Richard C. Atkinson served from 1995-2003 as the seventeenth president of the University of California system. His eight-year tenure was marked by innovative approaches to admissions and outreach, research initiatives to accelerate the University's contributions to the state's economy, and a challenge to the country's most widely used admissions examination—the SAT 1—that paved the way to major changes in the way millions of America's youth are now tested for college admissions. Before becoming president of the UC System, he served for fifteen years as chancellor of UC San Diego where he led that campus's emergence as one of the leading research universities in the nation. He is a former director of the National Science Foundation, past president of the American Association for the Advancement of Science, and was a long-term member of the faculty at Stanford University. His research in the field of cognitive science and psychology has been concerned with problems of memory and cognition. He is a member of the National Academy of Sciences, the Institute of Medicine, the National Academy of Education, the American Philosophical Society, and a mountain in Antarctica has been named in his honor.

Holly Harris Bane has been the associate vice president for strategic initiatives and engagement at the University of Akron, Ohio, since 2006. In this recently created position, she is responsible for aligning and leveraging the university's expertise in education, workforce training, and resource development to initiate new opportunities for strategic engagement that benefit the region, the state, and the university. She developed and now leads a university-wide Engagement Council comprised of a cross section of colleges and administrative units. She provides leadership for programs of educational outreach that are based on market research, workforce development trends and state and federal priorities. She has directed the development, construction, educational partnerships, and operation plan for the Medina County University Center—a $9 million, 33,000 square foot workforce development and innovation degree facility for secondary students and incumbent workers. Prior to assuming this post she served as director of strategic initiatives for the University of Akron from 2001-2006, where she was responsible for seeking opportunities for external engagement that align with the university's academic programs.

From 1999-2001, Ms. Harris Bane served in the Office of the Governor and the Ohio Department of Education, where she was responsible for the launch and implementation of Governor Taft's chief educational initiative to award $50 million in grants and recruit 20,000 volunteers to serve as reading tutors. She also created partnerships and collaborative opportunities to support the *OhioReads* initiative. Other responsibilities at the University of Akron have included the position of assistant director of the Ray C. Bliss Institute of Applied Politics (1989-1999). She received an M.A. from the University of Akron in political science, an M.A. in administration in higher education from Ohio State University, and has pursued Ph.D. work in Russian history from the University of Akron.

Thomas Bowles was appointed as science advisor for New Mexico Governor Bill Richardson in July 2006. As the science advisor, Bowles is responsible for providing advice to the governor on science and technology (S&T) issues, integrating S&T activities across New Mexico, and working with the national laboratories, universities, and industry in New Mexico to advance collaborations and couple advances in S&T into the public sector. Prior to his appointment as science advisor, Bowles served for two years as the chief science officer of Los Alamos National Laboratory. In that role, he was responsible for oversight of the full range of science carried out at the laboratory. Those responsibilities included serving as a member of the senior executive board, having oversight for more than $100M a year in discretionary research funds, having oversight over all external scientific reviews and strategic science planning, serving as the laboratory's principal contact with universities and other institutions, and ensuring the vitality of the scientific staff. Bowles came to Los Alamos in 1979 to establish an effort in weak interaction physics that has gone on to be recognized as one of the leading efforts in the world. He has been a key player in several international neutrino experiments and the principal investigator on a fundamental symmetries program. During his time at the laboratory, Bowles has served in a variety of positions and received a number of awards, including the M.A. Markov Prize that was awarded by the Institute for Nuclear Research of the Russian Academy of Sciences for his work as a principal investigator of the Soviet-American Gallium Experiment, a major solar neutrino investigation. In addition to being both a Laboratory fellow and a fellow of the American Physical Society, Bowles is an affiliate professor at the University of Washington. He has served on numerous laboratory and national committees, advisory panels, and editorial boards, including the Department of Energy and National Science Foundation's Nuclear Science Advisory Committee. Bowles earned his bachelor's degree in physics and mathematics from the University of Colorado and his doctoral degree in physics from Princeton University.

Jay Cole has served as the education policy advisor to West Virginia Governor Joe Manchin since January 2005. In this capacity, he advises the governor on both preK-12 and postsecondary education policy. From 2001 to 2005, he served as the deputy secretary of education and the arts and senior policy advisor in the administration of Governor Bob Wise. He is completing his Ph.D. in higher education and public policy at the University of Michigan, where his dissertation is a study of the diffusion of science and technology policy innovations across states. He holds an M.A. in educational policy and leadership from Ohio State University and a B.A. with honors in political science and history from West Virginia University. Jay is a 1993 Truman scholar, a 1995-1996 foreign language and area studies fellow, a Spencer Foundation fellow from 1996-2000, an international leader delegate to the European Union Visitors Program in 2005, and a 2007 Christine Mirzayan Science and Technology Policy Fellow at the National Academies. He is coauthor of a 2002 RAND monograph on higher education philanthropy and served as assistant editor of the *Association for the Study of Higher Education's 2001 Reader on Higher Education Finance*. His professional interests include higher education policy, state innovation, research, and economic development policies, international and comparative education, and the history of American education. He is a member of the steering and nominating committees of the Education Commission of the States and a member of the Southern Regional Education Board.

Marla Cone is one of the nation's premier environmental journalists. Cone has more than 20 years of experience covering environmental issues at the *Los Angeles Times* and other newspapers. She is author of the book, *Silent Snow: The Slow Poisoning of the Arctic*, published in 2005, which was a finalist in the National Academies' 2006 Communication Award. She has twice won a national award for environmental reporting. Her reporting at the *Times* focuses on environmental health issues. Cone earned a bachelor of arts in journalism and political science at the University of Wisconsin, Whitewater.

Edward G. Derrick directs the American Association for the Advancement of Science Research Competitiveness Program, which provides review, evaluation and guidance to the science and engineering community on the development of quality research programs. He has worked for the science and policy programs at AAAS since 1998, when he joined as a program associate. Derrick holds a Ph.D. from the University of Texas, Austin, with a dissertation in theoretical particle physics, and the science bachelor from MIT, with a thesis in biophysics. His academic experience includes two years at Humboldt University in Berlin as an Alexander von Humboldt fellow and his work experience includes one and a half years as a nuclear design engineer for Ontario Hydro. Ed's publications include papers in refereed scientific journals, conference proceedings, project reports, software documentation and newspaper articles.

Lynn Edward Elfner is chief executive officer of The Ohio Academy of Science, Columbus, where he also serves as acting editor of *The Ohio Journal of Science*. Previously he was with the Mt. Orab Local School District (science teacher), Ohio State University (instructor), the Ohio Environmental Council (executive director), and the Office of Budget and Management of State of Ohio. In January 1999 he was elected to the Board of Directors of the Washington, DC-based Triangle Coalition for Science and Technology Education. He is a former member of the Board of Directors, Ohio Scientific Education and Research Association. He is a fellow of the American Association for the Advancement of Science; he has received the Ohioana Book Award, Ohioana Library Association, 1980, Distinguished Service Award, National Association of Academies of Science, 1981, Distinguished Alumni Award, College of Agriculture, 1984, Honorary 100 from Ohio in Natural Resources, 1987, Centennial honoree, Herbarium, 1992, OSU, and Friend of Science Award, Science Education Council of Ohio, 1998; President's Award , the Ohio Alliance for the Environment, 2003. Current activities: ex officio member, Board of Trustees, the Ohio Academy of Science; ex officio member, Board of Trustees, The Ohio Historical Society; Board of Directors, archivist, and Academy representative, National Association of Academies of Science; past Chair, Central Ohio Technology Day Awards Committee; member of both the State Science Education Standards Advisory Committee and the Technology Education Standards Advisory Committee of the Ohio Department of Education; a member of the American Association for the Advancement of Science since 1969; a member of the National Science

Teachers Association; a member of the Ohio Historical Society, and a former member of the Ohio Society of Association Executives. In October 2003 he received the President's Award from the Ohio Alliance for the Environment. In November 2004 he received the President's Award from the Ohio School Boards Association. He received a B.S. in zoology and an M.S. in plant ecology from Ohio State University.

Kenneth R. Fulton is the executive director of the National Academy of Sciences. Following service in the U.S. Navy, where he was trained as a linguist, he joined the staff of the Academy in 1971. He served as administrative officer for the Office of Scientific Personnel, and then as program officer in the Food and Nutrition Board, coordinating several studies of the use and consumption of food additives for the Food and Drug Administration. In this capacity, he served for three years on the U.S. delegation to the Codex Alimentarius Commission of the United Nations. In 1980, he was appointed to the Academy's executive office, first as director of membership, then as special assistant to the president and executive director. Mr. Fulton's responsibilities include the Academy's membership and program activities, including the election of members and their annual and regional meetings; the offices of the Academy president and vice president and its governing Council; the National Academies *Keck Futures Initiative*; the Arthur M. Sackler colloquia and *Frontiers of Science* symposia; the Koshland Science Museum; and the *Office of Exhibitions and Cultural Programs*, which brings art exhibits and concerts to the Washington community. He is also the publisher of the *Proceedings (PNAS)*, the Academy's journal of original research, and executive director of The National Academies Corporation, which owns the Arnold and Mabel Beckman Center of the National Academy of Sciences and the National Academy of Engineering. He is a member of the American Society of Association Executives and the American Association for the Advancement of Science, and served on the Committee on Dissemination of Scientific Information of the International Council for Science. Mr. Fulton holds a bachelor's degree from the University of Maryland in the social and behavioral sciences, and a master's degree from American University in management.

Susan Hackwood is currently executive director of the California Council on Science and Technology (CCST), and professor of electrical engineering at the University of California, Riverside. CCST is a not-for-profit corporation comprised of 150 science and technology leaders sponsored by the key academic and federal research institutions in California, which advises the state on all aspects of science and technology including stem cell research, intellectual property, climate change, energy, information technology, biotechnology, and education. Dr. Hackwood received a Ph.D. in solid state ionics from DeMontfort University, UK. Before joining academia, she was department head of device robotics technology research at AT&T Bell Labs. In 1984 she joined the University of California, Santa Barbara as professor of electrical and computer engineering and was founder and director of the National Science Foundation Engineering Research Center for Robotic Systems in Microelectronics. In 1990, Dr. Hackwood became the founding dean of the Bourns College of Engineering at the University of California, Riverside (UCR). At UCR, she oversaw the development of all research and teaching aspects of five degree programs to the Ph.D. level. Dr. Hackwood's current research interests include science and technology policy, distributed asynchronous signal processing, and cellular robot systems. Dr. Hackwood has published over 140 technical publications and holds seven patents. She is a fellow of the Institute of Electrical and Electronics Engineers, Inc. (IEEE) and the American Association for the Advancement of Science (AAAS) and holds honorary degrees from Worcester Polytechnic Institute and DeMontfort University, UK. From 2003-2005 she was a visiting scholar at the Anderson School of Management, University of California, Los Angeles. In fall 2005 she was a visiting scholar at the California Institute of Technology. Dr. Hackwood has worked extensively with industry, academic and government partnerships to identify policy issues of importance to the country's citizens. She is also an active participant in regional and state economic development. With a strong interest in science and technology policy, Dr. Hackwood is currently involved with science and technology development in California, the United States, Mexico, Ireland, Taiwan and Costa Rica. She has been appointed as an honorary member of the Comision Asesora en Alta Tecnologia for Costa Rica and the California-Mexico Commission on Education, Science and Technology. In 2003 she was appointed a member of the AAAS Committee on Science Engineering and Public Policy and is the 2007 chair. From 2000-2002 she was a member of the AAAS Engineering Delegate and is currently chair of the Section on Societal Impacts of Science and Engineering. She is a member of the IEEE Spectrum Editorial Board. She has also served on the Board of Directors and consults on new product development for several electronics companies.

Bill Hammack is a professor of chemical and biomolecular engineering at the University of Illinois, Urbana-Champaign. He served a year as a diplomat at the U.S. Department of State (2005-2006) working as a senior science advisor for the Office of Korea Affairs and the Bureau of International Security and Non-Proliferation. He is the only engineering professor tenured for reaching out directly to the public. Since 1999 Bill has created over 300 pieces for public radio. He is a regular commentator on Marketplace, public radio premier business program, and was, for several years, the "resident engineer" on Radio National Australia's Science Show. For this work, he has been recognized by many journalistic, science and engineering societies. He has won the National Association of Science Writers' Science-in-Society Award, the American Institute of Physics Science Writing Award, the American Chemical Society's Grady-Stack Medal, the American Society of Mechanical Engineers' Church Medal, the IEEE Award for Distinguished Literary Contributions Furthering the Public Understanding of Engineering, the American Institute of Chemical Engineers' Service to Society Award, the American Society of Engineering Education's President Award, and the National Federation of Community Broadcasters' Silver Reel for National News and Commentary.

William C. Harris is president and CEO of Science Foundation Arizona. Dr. Harris went to Ireland as director general of Science Foundation Ireland (SFI) in 2001 and moved to Arizona in July 2006. Dr. Harris served at the U.S. National Science Foundation (NSF) from 1978 to 1996, including as the director from 1991-1996 for the Mathematical and Physical Sciences Directorate (MPS). In MPS, he was responsible for a federal grants appropriation of $750 million per year. At the NSF, he also established 25 science and technology centers to support investigative, interdisciplinary research by multiuniversity consortia. Earlier in his career, he catalyzed the Research Experiences for Undergraduates Program in the chemistry division and it became an NSF-wide activity. Immediately prior to going to Ireland, Dr. Harris was vice president for research and professor of chemistry and biochemistry at the University of South Carolina (USC), overseeing research activities throughout the USC system, several interdisciplinary centers and institutes, the USC Research Foundation, and sponsored research programs. Dr. Harris has authored more than 50 research papers and review articles in spectroscopy and in 1997 became a fellow of the American Association for the Advancement of Science. In 2004, he received the Wiley Lifetime Achievement Award from California Polytechnic State University. He was elected a member of the Royal Irish Academy in 2005. He earned his undergraduate degree at the College of William and Mary and his Ph.D. in chemistry at USC.

Doug Henton is president of Collaborative Economics. He has more than 30 years of experience in economic and community development at the national, regional, state, and local levels. Doug is nationally recognized for his work in bringing industry, government, education, research, and community leaders together around specific collaborative projects to improve regional competitiveness. He was project manager for the start-up of the Joint Venture: Silicon Valley Network, an innovative, results-oriented regional economic development alliance. Doug directed the strategic planning process involving more than 1,200 corporate, community, and public-sector leaders. He was a senior advisor for the *Silicon Valley 2010: A Regional Framework for Growing Together*. He continues to serve as Joint Venture's economist, and is the architect of Joint Venture's annual *Index of Silicon Valley*. Doug is a consultant to the California Economic Strategy Panel, California's first state economic strategy process linked to industry clusters and regions. He helped launch collaborative regional efforts in Sacramento and San Diego. He was consultant to the Massachusetts Technology Collaborative. Doug has also advised Chicago Metropolis 2020, the Potomac Conference and Arizona Partnership for a New Economy. Doug founded Collaborative Economics in July 1993 after a decade as assistant director of SRI International's Center for Economic Competitiveness. At SRI, Doug directed local strategy projects in diverse regions, including Austin, Texas. He led major state-level strategy development projects in Arizona, Florida, and California. Internationally, Doug directed major projects on the economic future of Hong Kong, the technopolis strategy in Japan, and regional development in China. With colleagues Kim Walesh and John Melville, Doug has written a book, *Grassroots Leaders for the New Economy: How Civic Entrepreneurs Are Building Prosperous Communities*, which was published by Jossey-Bass in March 1997. Their second book *Civic Revolutionaries: Igniting the Passion for Change in America's Communities* was published by Jossey-Bass in October 2003. Doug holds a bachelor's degree in political science and economics from Yale University and a master of public policy degree from the University of California, Berkeley.

John McDonald is president and owner of Stone's Throw, a strategic communications company providing advice and services to organizations engaged in issues impacting children, families and communities. With more than 20 years of communications experience, he brings considerable expertise to the campaigns and projects of his clients. He is particularly skilled in working with the news media, the development of strategic campaigns, and the creation of effective communication products in print, online, and video formats. Much of John's work at Stone's Throw has focused on issues related to public education, and public health. In the process he has helped philanthropic, academic, nonprofit and political organizations to effectively communicate with key audiences and to make policy makers and members of the news media more aware of the research, actions and opinions of his clients. A partial list of clients includes: the California Wellness Foundation, the California Family Health Council, the Center for the Future of Teaching and Learning, The Children's Partnership, the Cotsen Foundation, the Los Angeles Educational Partnership, the UC Berkeley—UCLA Health Insurance Policy Program, the University of Southern California Center on Philanthropy and Public Policy, among others. Prior to forming Stone's Throw, John was communications director for the Los Angeles Educational Partnership (LAEP), a nonprofit organization working for the reform of public education in Los Angeles. Through his efforts the organization received extensive national and local recognition, including coverage in *Fortune*, *NewsWeek*, *Los Angeles Times*, *New York Times*, and other major newspaper, television and radio news outlets. He also led the development of *Principal for a Day*, a special event that has become a school involvement model for communities across the nation. John was also press secretary to Leo McCarthy, Lieutenant Governor of California, and worked on the press and advance efforts of Mr. McCarthy's 1988 campaign for the U.S. Senate. He has also worked in other Democratic political campaigns including Tom Bradley's 1986 campaign for governor of California. Mr. McDonald also worked for the CBS local news affiliate (KCBS-TV) in Los Angeles and as a freelance writer. His writing has been published in the *Los Angeles Times* and other major publications.

Larry McKinney serves as director of coastal fisheries and senior director of aquatic resources, Texas Parks and Wildlife Department in Austin. He received his Ph.D. from Texas A&M University in 1976 and also was a Smithsonian summer fellow in 1976. From 1977 to 1980, he was a research associate/instructor at Texas A&M University at Galveston, 1977-1980 he was the director, of the Texas Environmental Engineering Field Laboratory, Galveston 1980-1986. In 1986 he came to the Texas Parks & Wildlife Department where he rose to the director of resource protection in 1988 and to senior director for aquatic resources in 1990. His programmatic responsibilities include a broad range of natural resource issues: water policy, coastal fisheries; assessing and securing freshwater inflows to estuaries; wetland conservation and restoration; endangered species conservation; and, other issues related to the ecological health of Texas aquatic ecosystems. He received the *Outstanding Public Service Award* from the Nature Conservancy in 1991 and was named the *Conservationist of the Year* by the Sportsmen Conservationists of Texas in 1992. American Fisheries Society, Texas Chapter named him the Outstanding Fisheries Worker for Administration in 2007.

Warren Muir is executive director of the Division on Earth and Life Studies of the National Academies. Chartered by the U.S. Congress in 1863 to honor top scientists, engineers, and doctors with membership, the National Academies are a nongovernmental, nonadvocacy, nonprofit national organization. Each year the National Academies produce hundreds of independent, authoritative, peer-reviewed reports on science and technology issues that have been requested and funded by federal, state, and local government programs and private foundations. The Division on Earth and Life Studies includes twelve boards that produce reports on all aspects of the environment; the life, geological and chemical sciences and technology; agriculture; natural resources; radiation; laboratory animals; as well as disasters. It also covers biological, chemical, radiological, and nuclear homeland security issues. From 1971-1977, he was senior staff member for environmental health for the Executive Office of the President, Council on Environmental Quality. Dr. Muir served at the U.S. Environmental Protection Agency (USEPA) from 1977 to 1981, as first deputy assistant administrator for testing and evaluation and then as director of the office of toxic substances. From 1981 until he joined the staff of the Academies in 1999, he was president of the Hampshire Research Institute and of Hampshire Research Associates, Inc. and was principal investigator and/or author on many studies on risk assessment, pollution prevention, toxic chemicals in commerce, and environmental data. During that time he also was a member of the adjunct faculty of the Johns Hopkins School of Hygiene and Public Health. Prior to joining the staff of the National Research Council, Dr. Muir chaired two NRC committees and was a member of three others. In 2003, Dr. Muir received the National Academies Community Service Award. In 1992, HRH Queen Elizabeth conferred upon him the title Officer Brother (O.St.J.), and in 1996 the rank of Commander (C.St.J.) in The Most Venerable Order of St. John of Jerusalem. In 1992, he was part of a team that won the USEPA's Award for Pollution Prevention and the, USEPA Region 2 Pollution Prevention Award. Dr. Muir received the USEPA Outstanding Service Award in 1980. Dr. Muir is on the board of U.S. nonprofit friendship/peace organizations active in Northern Ireland, Cyprus, and Turkey. Warren received his B.A. from Amherst College. He was awarded M.S. and Ph.D. degrees from Northwestern University in chemistry. He has postdoctoral training in epidemiology from the Johns Hopkins University.

Matthew C. Nisbet is assistant professor in the School of Communication at American University, Washington, DC. A social scientist who studies the nature and impacts of strategic communication, his current work tracks scientific and environmental controversies and examines the interactions among experts, journalists, and various publics. In this research, Nisbet studies how news coverage reflects and shapes policy, how strategists try to mold public opinion, and how citizens make sense of controversies. He has analyzed a wide range of debates, including those over stem cell research, global warming, intelligent design-creationism, plant biotechnology, and hurricanes. The author of numerous research articles, his work appears across a number of leading peer-reviewed journals. Over the past four years, these studies have been cited more than a 170 times by other scholars. Nisbet tracks current events related to strategic communication at his blog Framing Science. Hosted by Seed Media Group, *Framing Science* was recently recognized by the *New York Daily News* as one of the Web's top political blogs. At American University, Nisbet teaches courses in political communication, communication and society, graduate research, and communication theory. He was previously on the faculty at Ohio State University and he has also taught at Cornell University and Dresden Technical University, Germany. Nisbet is a frequently invited lecturer at conferences and meetings across the United States and Canada, and he is often called upon for his expert analysis by major news organizations.

Leonard K. Peters has been with Battelle of Columbus, Ohio, since April 2003. From 2003 to 2006, he was director of the Pacific Northwest National Laboratory. As a Battelle vice president, Dr. Peters focuses on leveraging Battelle's longstanding efforts in science and math education, and in defining Battelle's partnerships with universities in the area of ultra high-speed, broad-bandwidth networking for research and education purposes. Prior to this role, Dr. Peters was the director of Pacific Northwest National Laboratory (PNNL), which is operated by Battelle for the U.S. Department of Energy and is located in Richland, Washington. He served as director from April 2003 through December 2006. At PNNL, Dr. Peters guided the laboratory of more than 4,000 staff to many successes, including an improved safety and security culture, significant increases in business volume, and enhanced relationships with regional research universities. Dr. Peters came to PNNL after serving as vice provost of research and dean of the graduate school at Virginia Polytechnic Institute and State University. While at Virginia Tech, Dr. Peters managed its diverse research and graduate education programs, ranging from biotechnology and materials to transportation and information technology. As the senior executive responsible for the Research Division, he started a unique program to stimulate and nurture interdisciplinary research. He initiated numerous public-private partnerships, such as between Carilion Health Services, Virginia Tech, and the University of Virginia to create the Carilion Biomedical Institute. Dr. Peters also served as president and chairman of the board of Virginia Tech Intellectual Properties, Inc. (VTIP), a university-affiliated nonprofit corporation. VTIP handles, protects, and licenses technologies developed by faculty, students, and staff at Virginia Tech. He chaired the Committee on Research of the Virginia Research and Technology Advisory Commission. Nationally, Dr. Peters also served as chair of the Council of Graduate Schools and Oak Ridge Associated Universities. Prior to his tenure at Virginia Tech, Dr. Peters spent nearly two decades with the University of Kentucky. He began there in 1974 as assistant professor of chemical engineering, progressing to his last assignment as acting vice president for research and graduate studies. In addition to faculty and management assignments, Dr. Peters has a distinguished career as a researcher in atmospheric chemistry. His leadership in research and management has earned Dr. Peters many honors and awards, including a 1990 National Science Foundation Award in Recognition of Contributions to Science and Technology in Kentucky. In March 2004, Dr. Peters received the Oak Ridge Associated Universities' Outstanding Leadership Award. Dr. Peters is a member of the Air and Waste Management Association, the American Association for the Advancement of Science, the American Association for Aerosol Research, the American Institute of Chemical Engineers, the American Society for Engineering Education, and Sigma Xi. He recently served on the Advisory Board for Washington State University's College of Engineering and Architecture, the Board of Directors for Heritage University (Toppenish, WA), the Board of Directors of the Kadlec Health System, Washington Technology Alliance, Washington Roundtable, and Washington State University Research Foundation; and currently serves on the Board of Directors for VITEX Systems, Inc. and the University of Pittsburgh College of Engineering's Mascaro Sustainability Advisory Board. Dr. Peters earned his B.S., M.S., and Ph.D. from the University of Pittsburgh in chemical engineering where he was recognized as a Distinguished Alumnus in 1997.

Karl S. Pister is chair of the governing board of the California Council on Science and Technology and chancellor emeritus of the University of California, Santa Cruz. Prior to retirement he completed five decades of service to higher education, beginning as assistant professor in the Department of Civil Engineering at University of California, Berkeley. He served as chairman of the Division of Structural Engineering and Structural Mechanics before his appointment as dean of the College of Engineering in 1980, a position he held for 10 years. From 1985 to 1990 he was the first holder of the Roy W. Carlson chair in engineering. From 1991 to 1996 he served as chancellor of University of California, Santa Cruz. From 1996 to 2000 he served as senior associate to the president and vice president-educational outreach in the University of California Office of the President. He has a Ph.D. in theoretical and applied mechanics from the University of Illinois, Urbana-Champaign.

Matt Sundeen is an attorney and program principal in the Environment, Energy Transportation Program of the National Conference of State Legislatures (NCSL). At NCSL, Matt tracks a wide variety of topics and coordinates NCSL's Science and Technology in Public Policy initiative. He has authored numerous reports and policy briefs, frequently appears on radio and television and has been widely quoted in news publications. Before he came to NCSL, Matt practiced law in Boulder, Colorado. Matt received his law degree from the University of Denver and a B.A. in international studies from Michigan State University.

John R. Unger II is a member of the senate of West Virginia. After graduating from Martinsburg High School with honors, Unger began his higher education career at West Virginia University (WVU). During his tenure at WVU, Unger studied biology and liberal arts as a University Honors Scholar and Phi Beta Kappa's Albert Lee Strum Scholar. There, he also immersed himself in many community and religious projects, including the establishment of the Employment and Training Program, which he also later established in Hong Kong as a missionary of the Evangelical Lutheran Church in America. These projects consequently began his extensive involvement in community interests. From 1988 to 1990, Unger worked for the United States Refugee Program as the Special Assistant to the Director in Hong Kong. There, he worked with Vietnamese refugee children to establish a secure and nurturing environment. John Unger took a year's leave of absence from WVU to work with Mother Teresa in Calcutta, India, during the monsoons and riots in 1990. There, he coordinated the distribution of relief supplies. He also served as a member of the International Rescue Committee and the U.S. State Department Disaster Assistance Response Team providing relief for Kurdish refugees in southern Turkey and northern Iraq following the Persian Gulf War. Upon his return to WVU, John Unger was awarded the United States Presidential Certificate of Merit for national service. Governor Gaston Caperton appointed him to serve on the National and Community Service Advisory Board from 1991 to 1993. As a board member, he helped in the planning and establishment of the West Virginia Institute for Service Learning. John Unger also helped to establish the West Virginia Campus Compact and WVU's Office of Service-Learning Program. When disaster hit, Senator Unger assisted with organizing the West Virginia Students United Relief in Florida following Hurricane Andrew. During that time, he coordinated the relief and reconstruction efforts of 120 volunteers. In December 1992, John Unger was named WVU's twenty-fourth Rhodes Scholar. This distinguished award, established in 1903 by Cecil Rhodes and given annually to 32 scholars nationwide, grants the recipients a two-year study program at Oxford University. He graduated from WVU with a B.A.in biology and liberal arts in 1993 and received his M.A. in economics and economic development from Oxford University. From 1994 to 1995, John Unger returned to Hong Kong, where he served as political advisor to the Hong Kong Legislative Council. There, he advised and assisted Legislative Councilors on local and international issues and governmental policies. He was extensively involved with the legislation that established Hong Kong's highest court, the Hong Kong Court of Final Appeal. Unger also served as Deputy Secretary to JUSTICE (The Hong Kong Section of the International Commission of Jurists). During that time, he was instrumental in establishing the Hong Kong Human Rights Monitor and advocating for other human rights legislation prior to the territory's hand over to the People's Republic of China in 1997. Returning to the United States in 1995, John Unger became engaged in economic development initiatives and remained very active in his community. He was vice president of Van Wyk Enterprises in Martinsburg, West Virginia from 1996-1998; founder and former president of the West Virginia International Trade Development Council, an organization made up of three economic development authorities in the Eastern Panhandle (Berkeley, Jefferson, and Morgan Counties) that strengthen economic ties between the tri-county region and other countries; founder of the Employment and Training Search Program, the Office of Service Learning at West Virginia University, the West Virginia Campus Compact; a founding Trustee to the Mountain Milestone Summer Day Camp for Mentally and Physically Disabled Youth in West Virginia; founding member of the Board of Directors for the Interfaith Volunteer Caregivers of Berkeley and Morgan Counties; former Chairman of the Disaster Assistance Team–Berkeley County American Red Cross and member of the Disaster Assistance Team; Board of Directors for the Jefferson County American Red Cross; Habitat for Humanity; Family Resource Network for the Eastern Panhandle; EVAK K9 Search and Rescue Team; United Way of Berkeley and Morgan Counties; Chamber of Commerce; Martinsburg Rotary; Eastern Panhandle Business Association; and the West Virginia Farm Bureau. From April to July 2003, Senator Unger served as the director of communications for Save the Children International in Iraq. There, he helped coordinate humanitarian relief, recovery and reconstruction operations and information management. Senator Unger also focused on providing direct relief and recovery assistance to orphanages, children hospitals, senior care homes and homes for the mentally disabled. Senator Unger was first elected to the West Virginia Senate in 1998 at the age of 29—making him one of the youngest state senators in West Virginia history. He is currently serving his second four-year term. He is chairman of the Senate Transportation and Infrastructure Committee; vice chairman of the Senate Health and Human Resources Committee; chairman of the Senate Subcommittee on Workforce, Innovation and New Economy; and chairman of the Senate Subcommittee on Bio-Terrorism and Homeland Security. He is a ranking member of the Senate Finance, Education, Economic Development,

Agriculture and Interstate Cooperation Committees. He is an advisor to the U.S. Department of Energy's National Energy Technology Laboratory regarding homeland security and economic development. Also, he is producer and host of WEPM Panhandle Live, a public affairs radio talk show in the Eastern Panhandle.